the **little book** *of*
Big Ideas
for a

Happy & Healthy Marriage

An easy and effective way
to help your marriage last
a lifetime!

By Alex A. Lluch
Author of Over 4 Million Books Sold!

WS Publishing Group
San Diego, California

The Little Book of Big Ideas
for a Happy and Healthy Marriage

By Alex A. Lluch

Published by WS Publishing Group
San Diego, California 92119
Copyright © 2012 by WS Publishing Group

For Inquiries:
Log on to www.WSPublishingGroup.com
E-mail info@WSPublishingGroup.com

ISBN13: 978-1-936061-41-9

Printed in China

Table of Contents

Table of Contents

Chapter 1

Introduction

Couples who say "I do" have every intention of having a happy, healthy marriage. They want to live happily ever after; they want eternal marital bliss. They want someone they can count on through thick and thin. They want love, sex, friendship, partnership and companionship. And they want it for the rest of their lives. Indeed, having a successful marriage is one of the most rewarding experiences life has to offer.

Creating and maintaining a successful marriage is the result of many factors. Successful marriages are built from love, attraction, and compatibility. They require two people to honor, respect, and commit themselves to each other. They take a lot of work, some laughter, and at times, a bit of luck.

But creating the conditions required for a successful marriage has proven difficult for many Americans. About half of all first marriages and more than 60 percent of second marriages do not succeed. Marriages are challenged by a variety of factors in contemporary society. Unrealistic expectations of love and partnership is an example of such a challenge, one that is often fueled by the media. Indeed, movies and television tend to portray love, courtship, and marriage as carefree, passionate, romantic endeavors in which even the most unlikely or incompatible pair come together to find true love. While that's a lovely idea, the reality of love, compatibility, and marriage is often very different. Furthermore, it is quite telling that most romance movies end when a couple first falls in love — the story stops just when the relationship starts to require more complex conditions to succeed.

Consumer culture poses another challenge to successful marriage. We spend much of our time and energy acquiring material wealth, otherwise known as "stuff." When we are not out buying, we are watching advertisements for even more products — it is estimated that the average American is exposed to anywhere from 247 to more than 3,000 advertisements per day. With such a premium placed on materialism, our relationships suffer. Experts believe that materialism and consumerism encourage us to forget about the important things, which in turn causes us to drift from the people who enrich our lives.

Finally, many relationships struggle because couples lack the basic communication tools required to keep the marriage on track. Though it is something we do every day, communicating is a surprisingly difficult enterprise for most of us. Communication problems rank among the most common in not only romantic relationships, but professional, and familial ones as well. As a result, billions are spent every year on industries geared toward helping people improve their communication skills.

Good communication results in better relationships and more successful marriages. It can save you and your partner time, energy, and frustration. Think of how many times you and your partner have fought long into the night because he or she didn't understand your point, or because you weren't able to adequately express your feelings. Communication skills are not learned overnight, but they are able to be practiced by everyone who cares to learn them — and they are found right here in this book.

For these reasons and more, you'll find this book is an essential and practical handbook for couples of all ages, in all stages of marriage. This book is filled with ideas that are easy to understand and apply. The wisdom contained within helps couples nurture their relationship, create realistic expectations, and to grow within a partnership. To accomplish this, each chapter offers specific tips which address the most common pitfalls that create marital discourse and strife.

Why is a healthy marriage important?

There are many physical and emotional benefits to sustaining a healthy marriage. Statistics show that compared with unmarried people, married men and women have higher levels of happiness, self acceptance, and good health. They report greater satisfaction with their sexual lives and a general contentment not achieved by those who are unmarried. Furthermore, compared with unmarried people, married women and men tend to have lower levels of mortality, drug and alcohol abuse, isolation, depression, and risky behavior. In fact, being married decreases mortality rates by 50 percent for women and 250 percent for men. Finally, married people tend to earn more, save more, and have more assets than single people. For example, one recent study documented that married people in their 50s and 60s had an individual net worth roughly double that of divorcees, widows, or other unmarried people of the same age. Clearly, being successfully married contributes to a healthier, longer, and more fulfilling life.

Marriage also benefits society as a whole. Studies show that children from two-parent homes experience better emotional and physical health, higher success in school, and less tendency to abuse drugs and alcohol. Couples are more likely to participate in community and volunteer activities, thus enriching the local area. Finally, studies show that married individuals are more likely to earn higher wages and be more stable employees than unmarried people. Therefore, it is critical for society as a whole to create and sustain healthy and happy marriages.

What are the challenges of marriage today?

Most people get married because they fall in love and want to spend the rest of their lives together. Given this, one might assume that most people get divorced because they no longer love each other. However, quite the opposite is true; most people get divorced not because they no longer care for their spouse, but because they grow dissatisfied with and disconnected from their relationship.

But even if a marriage appears broken, there is usually plenty to salvage. Unfortunately, couples who are equipped only with a starry-eyed, impractical model of marriage are easily dismayed when their marriage hits a rough patch. Not realizing they can work through their problems to achieve a more satisfying union, more than half of all couples divorce, switch partners, and remarry—with even worse odds of success.

What are we doing wrong?

There are many mistakes people make in their marriages, but research shows most couples commonly make two of them: failing to communicate and failing to maintain a connection with each other. Simply put, couples don't know how to relate on a day-to-day basis, and have trouble staying connected through the years. In fact, couples are so consistent in their inability to succeed in these areas that experts call them "predictors for divorce."

Although more than half of all couples end up divorced, you can make it a priority to avoid this unhappy ending.

There are many reasons not to divorce: in fact, divorcing can be counted high on the list of things couples commonly do wrong! Divorce takes a heavy emotional and financial toll on a family. Research shows that after a divorce, depression rates rise and financial stress greatly increases. It also hits the wallet hard: according to one reputable marriage web site, divorce is a $28-billion-a-year industry that costs the average individual about $20,000. If the marriage produced children, divorce is even more costly, as child support payments will likely be required. Divorce is also costly to our government. Studies show that a single divorce can cost the state and federal government approximately $30,000. Divorce results in higher use of food stamps and public housing and causes an increase in juvenile delinquency and bankruptcies. In 2002, there were 10 million divorces in America, which is estimated to have cost taxpayers almost $30 billion.

While 82 percent of married couples will make it to their fifth anniversary, only 33 percent will make it to their 25th anniversary. The aim of this book is to improve those odds. To have lasting love and companionship, this book helps you develop the perspective, attitude, and tools for a healthy and successful relationship. Our goal is to bring ongoing joy to already happy couples and a renewed sense of love and commitment to couples that are struggling. Love is out there—go and get it!

Chapter 2

Maximizing the Benefits of This Book

Always keep this book handy. Keep it in your briefcase or purse. Put it in the glove box of your car. Stick it in the top drawer of your desk at work. Keep it on your night stand or in your gym bag. This book is meant to be read over and over again, and to do that, you will need to have it handy.

Be open to implementing the ideas in this book in your everyday life. Find tools that work well for you and your partner, and practice the principles as often as you can. Remember, it will take time, patience, and diligence to create a successful marriage that incorporates love, trust, and compromise. But have faith that you and your spouse can learn to achieve a happy, healthy marriage for life.

Chapter 3

Cultivating Trust

Trust is an integral part of every healthy and successful relationship. It is the foundation of intimacy, the doorway to commitment. Trust means having confidence that your spouse will treat you fairly, honestly, and responsibly. Trust takes years to build, and means different things to different couples. Some couples build trust through traveling and having extraordinary experiences together; others build trust through fidelity; still others build trust by showing each other sides of themselves that no one else may know.

Cultivating trust in your marriage has many benefits. Only with trust can real love take root. When you trust your partner, you experience a healing sense of comfort, safety, and intimacy. Trust also allows you and your spouse to confidently tackle marriage's challenges together, such as making harrowing financial decisions or raising children.

Although trust is an important piece to any relationship, it is easy to break and difficult to rebuild. Indeed, trust is delicate. It can be damaged in mere moments, and can take months, or years, to repair.

For those who have had their trust broken once, it may not come back easily. But even if you have been hurt in the past, it is possible to learn to trust again. It is also vital that you do: relationships that lack trust also lack intimacy, safety, and true love. Though it can be scary, trusting reaps rich rewards in relationships. As the American painter Walter Anderson once said, "We're never so vulnerable than when we trust someone—but paradoxically, if we cannot trust, neither can we find love or joy."

If you want to enjoy a healthy and successful marriage, you must learn two things: to trust your spouse, and to be trustworthy yourself. Use the following simple principles to build trust in one another over time, mend trust when it is damaged, and acknowledge the difficulties of trusting your spouse. By cultivating trust, you will be one step closer to making your marriage a success.

1

Make sure your words and actions match.

Marriage and love require honesty and credibility to be successful. In other words, in order to be trusted, you must be the kind of person who does what they say they will do. In your marriage, this means coming home from work when you say you will. It means following through when you plan to do something or be somewhere. If you are unsure you'll be able to back your promise up with action, don't promise it. Your loved one will be more disappointed should you break a promise than if you never make one in the first place. An atmosphere of trust is created only when your words are consistent with your actions.

Don't keep secrets from your spouse.

Sometimes married people hide things from one another. A husband may play a round of poker with some buddies and choose not to mention it to his wife. A wife might treat herself to a night at the movies or an afternoon massage and "forget" to tell her husband. These secrets seem harmless, but they put a small barrier between you and your spouse. Furthermore, little secrets can lead to bigger secrets, such as making friends, purchases, or other big decisions your spouse may not approve of. Should such secrets surface, they erode trust between you and your partner. Being open shows your spouse that you value honesty and that the lines of communication, which are vital to trust, are open.

Progress through the five stages of trust.

Developing trust is a complex process that doesn't happen overnight. Instead, you and your partner are likely to move through several stages of trust over the course of your marriage. Experts have identified five such stages. First comes the willingness to trust. Second, you must become aware of any personal history that may make 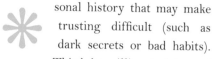 trusting difficult (such as dark secrets or bad habits). Third, be willing to let go of resentment and jealousy, which erode trust. Fourth, be patient if you or your partner backslide; trusting means having faith now and then. Finally, relish moments which reflect the depth of you and your partner's trust.

Create a trusting atmosphere.

To foster trust, you and your spouse must feel you are able to speak freely about concerns, problems, fears, and issues without being criticized, judged, or attacked by the other person. Criticism and judgement will only put your spouse on the defensive and make him or her afraid to speak up the next time. Therefore, a critical part of nurturing trust in your relationship is creating an atmosphere where both you and your spouse feel safe and comfortable, even when problems or concerns arise. As trust builds, you will find it easier to communicate with each other. Once the lines of communication between you and your spouse are open, you will be able to combat any problem or work through any issue together.

5

Don't allow jealousy to destroy trust.

The number one enemy of trust is jealousy. Married people will feel jealous if they are insecure about their relationship. Thus, you might feel jealous of your husband's attractive co-workers, or worry that your wife finds her trainer sexier than you. More often than not, jealousy is a product of paranoia and is not based on fact. Indeed, the inability to trust your partner with others, stems largely from insecurity. Sadly, the person who suffers most is you. As the author William Penn once noted, "The jealous are troublesome to others, but a torment to themselves." Don't torture yourself with feelings of jealousy; replace them with feelings of trust.

Know that rebuilding trust takes both of you.

Rebuilding trust once it has been damaged is difficult, and not always possible. If you have broken trust or been betrayed, the following steps will help mend trust between you and your partner. First, recognize your part in what went wrong. Second, allow space to express feelings, even if they may hurt. Be patient—you or your spouse may need to ask questions and process emotions repeatedly. Third, decide to forgive or be forgiven. This does not mean the incident is instantly forgotten; it is simply the first step toward healing. Finally, commit yourself to doing better in the future, which involves proving to your partner that you are trustworthy.

Have patience with trust.

Building and rebuilding trust doesn't happen overnight. Think of trust between partners as a city. Most of the world's grandest cities are also its oldest; a city's culture, buildings, infrastructure, and population have each been refined over decades, even centuries. Corners of Boston were the sites of historic battles; pockets of Paris witnessed some of the most important artistic movements in all of human history. So too will the trust that binds your relationship need to be honed and finetuned over months, years, even decades. To build such a thing, both you and your partner will need to have patience with trust. Trust does not develop quickly, but it can be enjoyed for a lifetime.

Know that trust is a leap of faith.

Trusting another human being is a risky endeavor. Any time we let someone in, we run the risk of getting hurt. However, we also take the chance of allowing ourselves to experience a deep, loving connection. To achieve this, you must have faith and trust. Martin Luther King Jr. once said, "Faith is taking the first step even when you don't see the whole staircase." Even though you have no guarantees, it is better to trust in the likelihood that your partner won't hurt you than to spend your whole relationship guarding against the possibility that he or she will. Not trusting your partner may make you feel safer in the short-term, but it will rob you of the opportunity to experience real love and intimacy.

Consider whether your past has diminished your ability to trust.

Sometimes trust issues have less to do with the current relationship a person is in and more to do with damage that may have occurred in childhood or past relationships. It takes courage to be willing to look into a painful past. You may need the help of close friends, or even a professional therapist, to guide you through this process. It is essential to a healthy marriage that you become aware of the source of your distrusting feelings. The only way to engage in a trusting relationship is to discard old baggage. Addressing mistrust from the past allows you to experience complete trust in the present.

Create a vault in which you and your spouse can put your trust.

The television show Seinfeld coined the phrase, "The Vault." If a character said, "Put it in the vault," it meant that the information should never get out to anyone else, no matter what. In other words, the vault was a pact of absolute solidarity. Create a vault in which you and your spouse can put your deepest secrets, fears, hopes, and dreams. Offer yourself as a secure vessel in which your spouse can confide his or her problems. Keep these secrets in confidence. If you become a vault for your partner, he or she will return to you again and again as a source of comfort and security— and will be there for you when you need the same.

Chapter 4

Creating Realistic Expectations

An expectation, simply put, is the understanding or belief that something particular will happen. Expectations play a large role in marriage. A wife may expect that her husband will show interest in her hobbies; a husband may expect his wife to do specific chores. But sometimes, when situations do not unfold as hoped, expectations serve as false guidelines. An expectation unmet feels like a broken promise and results in similar emotions: disappointment, frustration, even betrayal. In fact, of the 50 percent of marriages that end in divorce in their first 7 years, experts attribute many to unrealistic expectations that people have when they marry.

The goal in every marriage should be to have solid and realistic expectations. Having low expectations is not productive—when a person has low expectations they tend to underestimate their partner and disrespect themselves. Having overly high expectations, however, can set you up for failure. Expecting something of someone that they have not promised, or have no way of delivering, ensures that you will be disappointed.

Mark Twain once wrote, "Climate is what we expect, weather is what we get." In other words, when crafting expectations, it is important to have a realistic understanding of what you are likely to receive. Examine the expectations you have of your partner and consider whether they are realistic. Suppose you expect a clean house that functions peacefully at all times. Your partner will probably not be able to provide this for you. What your partner can do is offer to help when and where he or she is able, or to come up with alternative solutions (such as paying for a house-keeper). Maybe your full expectations (perfect order) won't be met, but some of your needs (a calmer, more orderly home) certainly can be.

Creating realistic goals means having high but healthy expectations. Allow the following principles to help you set your marriage up for success with real-istic expectations.

Don't expect perfection.

Human beings are flawed. As a result, it is almost guaranteed that your partner will possess at least one personality trait that you find disappointing. Expecting perfection from your partner will only frustrate you, and your partner will be angry and even hurt when held up to your unrealistic demands. Instead of perfection, expect flaws and foibles along with the good stuff. Focus on and be thankful for your spouse's positive traits. This attitude sets the stage for a love based on acceptance rather than false expectation. As author George Orwell wrote, "The essence of being human is that one does not seek perfection." Remember, if you seek perfection in your partner, your partner will seek it in you—and both of you are bound to be disappointed.

Expect bumps along the road.

Research shows that couples who expect to encounter marital challenges are more apt to face them successfully. In fact, studies reveal an almost direct correlation between marital success and the expectations that the couple had when entering the union. Simply put, if you expect a perfect ride, you are bound to be stalled by challenges. But if you head into your marriage expecting to encounter bumps along the road, you'll be more prepared to navigate your way. Be aware that marriage is a winding journey filled with some rocky, rainy moments. Succeeding in marriage means expecting to weather some storms now and then.

Make yourself happy first.

A common marriage myth is that it is your spouse's job to make you happy. Not only is that an unfair expectation, but it is a recipe for disaster. True happiness is an inside job. It occurs when you are at peace with yourself and your surroundings. Never enter into a relationship thinking it is going to become the sole source of your happiness. If you put that responsibility onto others, they will let you down over and over again. Relationships should enhance your happiness, not serve as its sole source. Depending on any one person for your happiness will leave you feeling disappointed and unfulfilled. As Lucille Ball said, "Love yourself first, and everything else falls into line."

Don't expect to do everything together.

Some couples fear that spending time apart will cause them to grow apart. More often, however, the opposite is true. Spending time apart can actually help a couple feel closer during the time they do spend together. A person who has their own friendships, hobbies, projects, and interests has a more enriched life. This person tends to be more self-confident, interesting, and well-rounded than others. Furthermore, having your own space breeds attraction between people. It fosters the very conditions that led you to fall in love with your partner in the first place. So don't be afraid to have a life outside of your partner. You may just find your spouse pulling you closer at night because he or she missed you during the day.

15

Acknowledge gender differences.

Men and women are wired differently, both genetically and psychologically. Nature has programmed us to think, feel, and react in different ways. Although there are exceptions to the rule, women tend to think and react with their hearts, whereas men tend to think and react with their heads. A woman's sense of self is often defined by her ability to connect, nurture, and maintain relationships. A man's sense of self is often defined by his ability to acquire skills and achieve results. These gender differences should be taken into account when crafting expectations for your partner. It is unreasonable to expect your wife or husband to deny their gender as they navigate the relationship.

Expect that you will disagree.

Another big marital myth is that happy couples agree on the big issues in their lives. To the contrary, research shows that almost 69 percent of the big issues, such as religion, child rearing, finances, and intimacy, are merely managed by partners, not necessarily solved. In fact, marital experts note that some couples argue about the same issues at their 20th anniversary that they argued about as newlyweds! Happy couples, however, learn to manage their disagreements through compromising rather than expecting to always agree. The reality is that sometimes you and your spouse will simply see an issue differently. Agreeing to disagree can be a handy tool in this case.

Expect that your marriage will change.

It has been said that the only sure thing you can predict in a marriage is that it will change. The nature of life, and of your marriage, is that each person is a work in progress, an infinitely evolving being. Change can be scary, but preventing your marriage from changing can significantly damage it. Expecting your marriage to change is a must for maintaining a strong and healthy bond. As author George MacDonald once said, "One of the good things that comes of a true marriage is that there is one face on which changes come without your seeing them; or rather there is one face which you can still see the same, through all the shadows which years have gathered upon it."

Know that marriage takes work.

Many newlyweds mistakenly believe that a wedding means an automatic "happily ever after." Well, there's a reason why we don't see this part in fairytales. You have to work on your marriage, just like you do with any other relationship. But think of this as part of the excitement! Coasting by would be boring. Remember, you need to nurture marriage and put energy into it. When problems arise (which, of course, they will), you'll have to address them and find solutions. If life gets hectic, remember to get creative and find ways to put the spark back into your relationship, such as weekly date nights. Adhere to David Mace's philosophy: "Love must be fed and nurtured, constantly renewed."

Expect your romance to have peaks and valleys.

Journalist Judith Viorst once said, "One advantage of marriage is that, when you fall out of love with him or he falls out of love with you, it keeps you together until you fall in again." Indeed, marriages go through many phases, some up and some down. Avoid questioning your love during down times. While wild passion is often a first indication you are in love, its lack doesn't mean you have fallen out of love. Many couples mistakenly fear that their spark has died, when in reality they are just in a down phase. You can help keep your marriage strong by navigating troubled times with patience and confidence.

Know that your partner is not a mind reader.

Simply because someone knows and loves you doesn't mean they will automatically understand your needs, wants, and desires. But many people mistakenly expect their partner to intuit their needs. Expecting your needs to be met without clearly stating what they are is passive aggressive. It sets your partner up for a test he or she cannot possibly pass. No matter how intense the love or how long the romance, you must express yourself out loud. Words to live by: If you want it honored, make it known.

Chapter 5

Showing Love Through Appreciation

In a marriage, appreciation must be expressed often. Heartfelt expressions of thanks for our spouse's good qualities, loving care, and small deeds send the message that you do not take your partner for granted. Successful couples appreciate one another out loud, and do so often.

Yet the majority of couples have trouble showing their appreciation for their spouse as often as they should. Over the years, husbands forget to tell their wives that their cooking is restaurant-quality; wives feel tired of repeating how much they appreciate their husband's help with chores. Couples tend to reserve these shows of appreciation for early in the relationship, when everything feels new. As Prince Philip, the Duke of Edinburgh once joked, "When a man opens the car door for his wife, it's either a new car or a new wife."

But small, frequent measures of appreciation can have a lasting impact on a relationship. Couples who make an effort to appreciate each other often report higher levels of partnership, friendship, and sexual intimacy. Furthermore, showing appreciation creates a chain reaction of these goodies. As Cicero once said, "Gratitude is not only the greatest of virtues, but the parent of all others." When one spouse shows appreciation, it catches on. After a while, you will find that your kind words or deeds are being returned.

To assess how well you and your spouse show appreciation, consider how often you tell your husband you are proud of him. Think of the last time you told your wife she is valuable. Make a list of ways in which you've actively shown your partner how much you appreciate him or her. If you are like most American couples, your list is probably pretty short.

By focusing on what you appreciate about your partner, you grow the positive aspects of your marriage, encourage your spouse to continue exhibiting positive behaviors, and cultivate an atmosphere of giving. Use the following principles to better appreciate your partner. You will be pleasantly surprised at how the good in your marriage begins to grow!

Sing unsung praises.

French Actress Simone Signoret once noted, "Chains do not hold a marriage together. It is threads, hundreds of tiny threads which sew people together through the years." Think of daily thank you's as the equivalent of these tiny threads which keep you and your partner strong over time. Thanking your spouse for a job well done offers validation that lasts for days. Even though it may seem like a husband or wife's job to make dinner, empty the trash, and feed the dog, it is still wonderful to hear the words "thank you" after completing these tasks. When you skip these two simple words, your partner may become resentful of his or her day-to-day responsibilities. Aim to thank your partner for at least one thing each day.

Say thank you, even for the small things.

Is your spouse patient with the kids, a reliable friend, or always able to fix the computer? Does your partner nurse you to health when you have a cold, make amazing lasagna, or pay the bills on time every month? Can he or she make you laugh like no one else? If you answered yes to any of these questions, you have something to praise your partner for. Pay attention to your husband or wife's unique personality traits and admirable gifts. As one-half of a successful marriage, it is your privilege to receive these gifts, but your job to appreciate them. Show your appreciation for your spouse by singing out praises for qualities that might otherwise go unnoticed.

Do something completely unexpected.

Don't wait for a birthday, anniversary, or holiday to surprise your spouse with a loving email, beautiful flowers, or thoughtful gift. Injecting an unexpected show of appreciation into your spouse's daily routine lets him or her know how much you care. Leave a note in your husband's briefcase, drop off a hot lunch at your wife's office, or bring home your spouses's favorite movie when it is least expected. These unplanned gestures are a great way to show your spouse he or she is constantly on your mind, and that you enjoy going out of your way to make your loved one happy. Even a sweet card (when it's not a birthday) is a small thing that can make your spouse smile and feel appreciated for weeks on end.

Don't sweat the small stuff.

We've all heard the adage, "To err is human." Naturally, your spouse will not always do the right thing. He or she may forget to pick up your clothes from the dry cleaner or neglect to clean out the garage like you asked. While some omissions constitute big problems for a couple (such as continually neglecting to do these things, or forgetting something very important), more often than not, whatever your spouse forgot is no big deal. Instead of getting angry, just say, "No problem." By not sweating the small stuff, you give your partner much-needed room to be human. Your spouse will appreciate being let off the hook once in a while and will likely reciprocate the favor.

Stop and smell the roses.

In today's world, Americans speed through their lives in a mad dash to accomplish one task after another. We each have a seemingly endless list of tasks that need to be accomplished, phone calls and emails that need to be returned, and errands that need to be run. Traveling this fast makes it easy for your married life to whiz by in a blur. But it is difficult to appreciate what you don't have time to see. Therefore, slow down. Take time to appreciate the small and sometimes magical moments of everyday life together. Push the pause button on your busy schedule, and spend a concentrated chunk of time appreciating your spouse. Slowing down allows you to realize how thankful you are for the person who is accompanying you on life's journey.

Find small ways to pamper your partner.

One way of keeping appreciation alive is to take time to accommodate the little things that mean so much to your spouse. Let your wife sleep in for an hour on the weekend. Hire a baby-sitter and take your husband out for a surprise dinner at his favorite restaurant. Do the dishes while your wife takes a long bubble bath. Set up a poker night for your husband and a few of his friends. Rabbi Barnett R. Brickner once said, "Success in marriage does not come merely through finding the right mate, but through being the right mate. " With this in mind, practice being a good mate by spoiling the one you love.

Write a gratitude list and place it where your spouse can see it.

In a recent study that ranked the reasons why most marriages fail, "no longer in love" placed second. Yet many people who think they are no longer in love with their spouse in reality just crave to be appreciated. Take the first step by making a list of things you appreciate in your partner. Your list can consist of sweet, funny, even gushy sentiments that express reasons you love your partner. Write things like, "You are a wonderful kisser," "You make the most delicious coffee," "You have sexy legs," or "You bring home pizza when I'm too tired to cook." After you complete your list, put it in a surprising place where your loved one will discover it.

Honor and validate your partner's dreams.

One surefire way to cultivate an atmosphere of appreciation in your relationship is to recognize your spouse's hopes, dreams, and hidden talents. Find what your spouse is passionate about; if he wants to paint, encourage him along the way. Buy him a canvas; praise the resulting work. If your wife wants to get a master's degree, help her make it a reality. Remind her how intelligent she is on a regular basis. Encourage your spouse to talk about his or her dreams. Give gentle nudges when he or she needs it. Assure your spouse you are there for support. By recognizing hopes and talents you are appreciating the shining star within your partner.

Appreciate the ways your partner grows and changes.

The entertainer Barbara Streisand once quipped, "Why does a woman work 10 years to change a man's habits and then complain that he's not the man she married?" Though Streisand was joking, she touched on a common sentiment: the failure of some partners to appreciate changes made by their spouse. When your partner successfully modifies his or her behavior, acknowledge it! For example, if you ask your spouse to hang up his wet towels and he finally starts doing it, tell him you appreciate his effort. If your wife finally starts buying the ice cream you like, thank her for being considerate. Positive reinforcement will encourage your spouse to continue the behavior.

Realize that unconditional love is the highest form of appreciation.

When you offer unconditional love and support to your spouse, you send a message of complete gratitude. You are telling your partner that he or she is good enough, does enough, and is enough. Unconditional love does not mean that you no longer see your spouse's flaws or accept behavior that is hurtful or wrong. Unconditional love means that you accept the entire package that is your husband or wife. You may even come to love the imperfections that make your spouse so unique. As the saying goes, "True love does not come by finding the perfect person, but by learning to see an imperfect person perfectly."

Chapter 6

Giving Affection

Humans are creatures that long to be touched and held. In fact, research has shown that for newborns, being touched is as critical as being fed! Studies of babies in orphanages and hospitals reveal that a lack of touch can result in severe weight loss, sickness, and even death. On the other hand, infants who are frequently touched gain weight faster, cry less, and experience more even vital signs than infants who are not touched. Our need to be touched doesn't stop at childhood: one study found that it takes at least 8 meaningful touches per day for an adult to thrive. Given these facts, it is no exaggeration to say that humans need to be shown affection in order to survive.

Affection is the outward expression of a person's love or fondness. People in affectionate relationships report feeling more love, closeness, and satisfaction than individuals in less affectionate relationships. Interestingly, affection has also been found to have health benefits. A study at Arizona State University's Hugh Downs School of Human Communication determined a strong correlation between being affectionate and having lower levels of stress and depression. The study also concluded that affectionate people are better equipped to deal with stressful situations.

Unfortunately, if you didn't grow up receiving affection regularly as a child, it may feel awkward or unnatural to show affection as an adult. But affection with your loved one is a language you can learn. Couples who devote just a few hours a week to being affectionate can have markedly improved relationships. Take small steps until you feel comfortable, such as holding hands while you take a walk. Snuggle in bed or while you watch a movie. Lovingly pat each other on the back while you give or receive a compliment.

There are many different ways to give and receive affection, and all healthy and successful marriages feature it in one form or another. Use the following simple principles to become a more affectionate partner to ensure the health of your relationship.

Lavish your spouse with compliments.

Even the most confident spouse needs to be reminded of his or her greatness at times. Complimenting your spouse is a simple way to make the person feel loved, valued, and desired. Express your affection by saying, "You look really attractive tonight," or "The dinner you made was delicious; you're such a great cook." Never assume your spouse already knows how attractive she is to you or what a good job he did painting the bedroom. Everyone needs and deserves validation from time to time; give it to your spouse in the form of affectionate compliments.

Recognize the power of touch.

Touch makes you feel physically and emotionally close to your partner. As a marriage goes on, spouses often let physical affection fall by the wayside. But touching goes a long way toward keeping married people healthy and strong. In fact, researchers at Wilkes University in Pennsylvania found that individuals who touch each other and have sex a couple times a week have 30 percent higher levels of an antibody called immunoglobulin A, which boosts the immune system. Sex is also reported to be a natural antihistamine, helping combat hay fever, asthma, and congestion. So touch your partner regularly—that, plus an apple, are sure to keep the doctor away.

Don't always equate affection with sex.

Being affectionate need not always lead to physical intimacy, although it certainly can. When you make a habit of showing physical affection without the implication that it must lead to sex, you increase the trust and intimacy between you and your partner. Interestingly, when trust and intimacy levels go up, physical affection tends to occur more frequently too. Above all, never let an agenda underscore your affectionate advances. If your affections lead to an intimate or sexual moment, that is wonderful. If they stop at a loving peck on the cheek or a heartfelt embrace, that too is to be cherished and appreciated.

Help each other heal.

If you or your spouse has a difficulty showing affection, don't blame each other — it may be the product of an unaffectionate past or growing up in an unaffectionate household. Being raised in a family where hugs and kisses were sparse is painful and can make demonstrating love through affection seem unnatural and uncomfortable as an adult. Help each other heal by starting small and not making the other person feel pressured. Acts of affection may feel awkward at first, but as you receive positive feedback, your comfort level will grow. Finally, consider talking with a therapist if you need extra help working through your issues. Everyone is capable of showing affection with the right support.

Don't withdraw affection, even if you get mad or frustrated.

It is a normal human tendency to withdraw affection when you are annoyed or irritated with your partner. But when you withhold affection as a result of being angry or frustrated, you in effect punish your partner in a physical way. It is important, therefore, not to establish what experts call a "punitive pattern of behavior," which is highly destructive to relationships. Although it may feel like a struggle, maintain loving contact, even when you and your spouse are in a disagreement. Not only will you avoid wielding intimacy as a punishment, but being affectionate can actually help most couples recover from many arguments.

Embrace pet names and private jokes.

Expressing your love through affection doesn't always have to be serious. Many happy couples create funny or silly pet names for one another, an act that shows fondness and fosters closeness between two people. Furthermore, most nicknames are born from endearing memories or a special inside joke. When you use your spouse's pet name, you'll both be reminded of a happy time. However, refrain from using mushy pet names in front of other people. Nicknames should be a fun, private thing, and your spouse may become embarrassed if his or her pet name is used in public. Keep the joke between you and your loved one and embrace the special feelings it creates.

37

Be playful together at least once a day.

Research shows that laughter promotes an actual chemical change in the body that can alleviate stress and ease pain. Indeed, laughter is truly a medicine that you and your spouse can take to reduce stress, tension, arguments, and improve your ability to feel affection for one another. Be playful by saying something lighthearted or silly to your spouse before he or she goes to work. Call in the middle of the day and share a funny story. Play like kids when you get home; sing, dance, and race each other to the bed. Toss a ball around outside. Go for a drive and make out like high schoolers in the car. The key is to do something silly and fun together and not to take life too seriously.

Make "for no reason at all" your motto.

Watch your spouse's face light up as you offer a lingering kiss for no reason at all when you pass in the hallway. Bring him or her a glass of cold lemonade on a hot day. Tidy up his or her desk, just because. Vacuum the inside of your wife's car, or fill up your husband's tank with gas. Bring home something that enhances your spouse's hobbies, such as new gardening tools, art materials, books, or running shoes. Offer meaningful pats and tender squeezes of affection at random. Unsolicited affection is a wordless way of saying: "You are on my mind, I appreciate you, and I want you to know." Watch how quickly these simple gestures of affection are reciprocated.

Don't keep score.

Katherine Hepburn once said, "Love has nothing to do with what you are expecting to get, only with what you are expecting to give, which is everything." But unhappily married couples often adopt an attitude of "I'll give when you do." They keep score of what they do for their partner, and of what their partner has done for them. Keeping score should never be part of a relationship, as it is not reflective of love and partnership. In successful couples, each person must be willing to give more than they get, and do so without comparing their efforts against their partner's. In this spirit, give affection, unsolicited and often, and remember that the more you put into your emotional bank account, the richer and fuller your marriage will be.

Decide that being together is your top priority.

In everyday life, your time as a couple can get pushed aside to make room for work, errands, and child-rearing. But marriages that are placed on the back burner tend to over-cook and spoil. Therefore, do at least one regular activity together. Partake in a couples' massage, go wine tasting, or attend a cooking class. Get season tickets to the theater or see a sports team you both love. Or, take a vacation: according to a 2006 study by Expedia.com, American workers collectively give back 175 million paid vacation days to their employers every year. If you are offered paid vacation, use it to treat yourself and your spouse to some quality time together.

Chapter 7

Sparking Romance

Author and journalist Mignon McLaughlin once said, "A successful marriage requires falling in love many times, always with the same person." Naturally, passion in a marriage will wax and wane, but romance can be just the thing to get a couple through the tough times. Many couples are surprised at how easy it is to be romantic, even after many years together. When both partners strive to be more romantic, you are truly strengthening your partnership and creating a bank of fond sentiments and memories.

But contemporary society can make maintaining the sparks in your marriage feel like hard work. With so much to do every day, most couples feel more tired than romantic by the end of the day. However, a married couple's capacity for romance is greater than one might think. In fact, a 2002 Seagram's national survey of American men found that married males are 14 percent more likely to prefer a romantic night than unmarried men. Even if it feels dormant, there is still likely to be romance between you and your partner.

To bring romance to the surface of your relationship, let go of any expectations or images of romance you currently hold. The notion of romance tends to conjure up images of elegant restaurants or white-sand beaches in foreign countries. Yet most romantic gestures need not cost a fortune or require extensive planning. Indeed, real romance is less about grand gestures and undying passion and more about small, intimate moments shared by you and your spouse. When you want to be romantic, let go of the idea that you are supposed to be doing anything other than a small, genuine gesture that lets your partner know you care for him or her very deeply.

Even if you fear the spark has already gone out of your marriage, the following simple principles will help you get it back. Decide to make romance a priority. Remember that opportunities for romance are found even in seemingly mundane moments. Use these and the following tips to rekindle the fire in your marriage.

Listen for hints.

If you listen, you'll likely notice your spouse dropping hints about how he or she would like to be romanced. Your partner might say something specific, such as, "I want to try that new restaurant," or, "I'd really love to go to Napa Valley for my birthday." Or, he or she might say something more general, such as, "Maybe it would be fun to take a walk sometime," or "I've been craving a good massage." Take note of these utterances, and act on them either in the moment or in the near future. Nothing will make your partner feel more special than if you demonstrate you were paying close attention. Just by listening, you can make your spouse's dreams a romantic reality.

Get outside your comfort zone.

Often, marriages struggle because one or both partners have fallen into a rut. After a while, couples are less interested in working at their marriages and putting time and effort into things like romance. In fact, a 2005 survey on marriage conducted by the National Fatherhood Initiative found that about 66 percent of divorced people say they wished they'd worked harder to save their marriages, and 62 percent wished their partner had worked harder. Don't wait to regret your marriage — be willing to work for your love. Go outside your comfort zone to show your partner you care. Go rock climbing if your spouse loves it, even if you are afraid. Try Indian food, even if you have a less adventurous palate. Your spouse will be attracted to your sense of adventure.

43

Dress for romance.

Inspire romance by dressing up when you see your spouse. With our hectic schedules, it can be tempting to throw on sweatpants or a ratty T-shirt after work. But resist the urge to lay around in yoga pants all weekend — it's comfortable for you, but not attractive to your partner. Instead, dress up as you would if you had a date with a new lover. Wearing a beautiful dress or a button-down shirt and slacks will be unexpected and make your partner feel special that you took the extra time to look nice. This goes for the bedroom as well; now and then, skip the dowdy nightshirt and wear something more exciting to bed. Taking time with your appearance inspires romance and shows your partner you care.

Make your spouse king or queen for a day.

Dedicate a day to pampering your spouse. First, absolve him or her from all duties, stressors, and chores. Fold the laundry while your spouse sleeps in. Serve breakfast in bed, treat your husband to a massage, or run a hot bath for your wife. Let your partner choose a nice restaurant for dinner or order from a favorite take-out spot. Shut out distractions by turning off your cell phone and email — this shows you are totally committed to giving your partner your complete attention on this special day. This selfless gesture will make your spouse feel loved and will make you feel proud of your ability to romance your partner.

Create anticipation throughout the day.

It is usually difficult to climb into bed after a long, hard day and get into a romantic mood. Indeed, after many years of marriage, romance does not always spark itself. Give it a boost by being romantic early in the morning, and keeping it going all day long. Slip a seductive note in your husband's briefcase. Whisper something sexy in your wife's ear just before you leave for work. Call your husband at lunch and remind him of a favorite romantic encounter. While making dinner, steal a moment and kiss each other sensually. By the end of the night, you'll both be rushing to bed.

Make a date once a week.

Successful couples create alone time and use it to nurture their partnership and reconnect during busy times. Spark romance with your partner by planning a date for just the two of you at least once a week. Whether you eat at your favorite Italian restaurant every Wednesday or spontaneously plan a picnic for a Sunday afternoon, stick to the once-a-week rule and don't waver. Avoid coming up with reasons why you are too busy or too tired; honor dates with your spouse as you would any other appointment you wouldn't cancel. After a few wonderful dates, you will find that date night becomes something you both look forward to all week long.

Indulge all five senses.

Romance is sensual, so enlist all five of yours to enjoy a full romantic experience. Indulge sight by bringing home an exotic plant or sparkling jewelry. Invoke smell by wearing special cologne, lighting a scented candle, or rubbing your spouse's shoulders with fragrant massage oil. Touch should be slow and sensual. Make it a mission to find hidden areas that give pleasure. To explore taste, use sensual foods like chocolate, berries, or champagne. Feed them to each other and savor the tastes and textures. To indulge hearing, play ambient music, read a poem out loud, or whisper sweet words in your spouse's ear. Romantic encounters that invoke all the senses are a more memorable and enjoyable experience.

48

Plan an escape.

According to a survey conducted by the travel company Expedia, 60 percent of couples feel that time away with their partners would improve their relationships. Taking a vacation is a perfect way to reconnect with your spouse. A change of scenery almost always cultivates romance. Getting away doesn't have to take lots of money or time—a night spent in a historic, local hotel, or a weekend devoted to exploring a nearby destination can be just as significant as an exotic beach vacation. The important thing is to get away and enjoy yourselves. Consider the wisdom of the Chinese proverb which says, "Vacations are not about 'getting away'—but about getting in 'touch.'"

49

Make your bedroom a sanctuary.

When your bedroom inspires peace and relaxation, romance is more likely to bloom. Your bedroom is the intimate space shared by you and your spouse, the site of your most personal and pleasurable moments. Do this sanctuary justice by treating it as such. Clear out clutter and remove unnecessary distractions. Reserve your bedroom for sleep and sex; do paperwork and watch TV in another room. Hang photos that remind you of happy times, such as your wedding day or a favorite trip. Invest in luxurious sheets and a soft comforter. Buy a small CD player and listen to music you both enjoy. Candlelight and a nice fragrance will also help the mood. Make your bedroom a private oasis for two.

Turn an ordinary occasion into a chance for romance.

Laziness and complacency are the enemies of a successful union. If you view every moment together as an opportunity for romance, your marriage will stay sharp. Avoid being lazy at all costs. Instead of paper plates in front of the television, set the dining room table with cloth napkins, fine dinnerware, wine glasses, and candles — no matter what is for dinner. Wear the beautiful necklace he gave you, even if you're only going to the movies. Don't wait for a special occasion —make one out of tonight. As journalist Mignon McLaughlin once wrote: "A first-rate marriage is like a first-rate hotel: expensive, but worth it."

Chapter 8

Being Spontaneous

Sociologist Helen Merrell Lynd said that spontaneity should be "an expression of our deepest desires and values." Being spontaneous in romance means being open to the adventure that marriage can be. It means suspending worry and being present and playful in your life. Furthermore, it means being open to using creativity to keep your relationship fresh, or being true to what Oscar Wilde meant when he wrote, "Marriage is the triumph of imagination over intelligence."

Without spontaneity, marriage falls into a routine. Marital boredom can be much like a car that runs on fumes — couples neglect to add gas to their car, yet are shocked when their marriage sputters to a stop. Being spontaneous with your partner takes you out of your comfort zone and helps you discover new interests. It is amazing how much trying a new recipe, hobby, sport, restaurant, or movie genre can open you and your partner up to each other.

In addition, spontaneity has impressive health benefits. Spontaneity helps reduce tension, stress, depression, and anxiety, all of which contribute to serious diseases and disorders, including cancer. This is why Dr. C. Robert Cloninger, M.D., author of Feeling Good: The Science of Well-Being, has said, "Spontaneous people have more positive emotions and greater satisfaction with life."

Yet many married people struggle with spontaneity because it means relinquishing control over a situation. When a day is unplanned, some of us worry something will go wrong. Others feel their time will be wasted if not carefully measured out in advance. Avoid worrying about these issues. Remember, there is always tomorrow to get errands done, and nothing bad is likely to happen if you and your partner wing it for a while.

Being spontaneous with your partner is nothing less than recapturing the youthful, exciting glow that helped you first fall in love. Use the following principles to create spontaneous moments in your marriage in order to keep your love fresh and new.

Be open to spontaneous moments.

A successful marriage requires partners to be creative. They must be open to discovering the opportunities for spontaneity that are everywhere. For instance, if you are walking with your spouse and pass a park that looks inviting, take your spouse's hand, lead him or her to a tree, and lounge for a while in the shade. If you see a festival, fair, or parade is happening in your neighborhood, pack up your family and just go. Should you drive by a beautiful beach, stop and stick your feet in the sand. Strive to be the kind of couple that is always willing to go on a small adventure at the spur of the moment. Remind yourselves that your regular life and all its demands will be there when you get back.

Surprise your spouse with a hug.

A spontaneous hug is a simple way to draw your loved one close and let him or her know you care. Give your spouse a hug when he or she least expects it — in the middle of dinner, in the middle of the night, while she is reading to the kids, as he is watering the plants — there are a thousand opportunities every day to steal a quick embrace. Hugs hold tremendous power — a 2007 study published by the National Institutes of Health found that "hugs and cuddles have long- term effects" on helping the brain, heart, and other major body systems. Indeed, hugs can bring you together for a brief romantic moment or slow you down when rushing from task to task. Best of all, hugs offer a chance for spontaneous physical closeness that you can have anytime, anywhere.

Act like kids again.

Studies show that laughter reduces stress, boosts the immune system, and fosters connection with others — yet adults rarely turn to laughter when they need to decompress. As children, humans laugh approximately 300 times a day; but when they become adults, that number drops to only 17 times a day, on average. As children, we were all more open to the moment, delighted by new things, and less self-conscious. Acting like kids again, no matter your age, is a great way to live in the moment without stress or fear. So, put on music and dance around, dust off that Frisbee, or play a board game. Go to the zoo or an amusement park. Promote health and happiness between you and your spouse by playing and laughing like children.

Go for a surprise drive down memory lane.

Nothing rekindles romance like revisiting a place where the fire was first lit. Arrange for an afternoon with your spouse, and use the opportunity to take a drive, but keep your destination a secret. Drive to a spot you frequented when your love was new. Offer hints about the destination and let your spouse guess. Nothing is sexier than an on-the-spot adventure that reminds you both of carefree times. British author Beverley Nichols once wrote, "Marriage is a book of which the first chapter is written in poetry and the remaining chapters in prose." Get back to the poetry that first sparked your relationship by taking a trip down memory lane.

Keep a bag packed.

Don't be kept from doing something fun and unplanned just because you are unprepared for it. This is especially important if you have young children who require snacks, diapers, and changes of clothing in order to do spontaneous activities. Plan for spontaneity by packing a bag that includes things like sneakers, sunscreen, water, towels, a jacket, and a swimsuit. Keep the bag in your car or at work, and you and your loved ones will be ready for a day at the beach or an impromptu hike at a moment's notice. Better still, you'll be teaching your family about the value of possessing a joy for life. Think of this bag as your emergency romance kit that allows you and your loved ones to have fun at the drop of a hat.

Rediscover your city together.

Next time you and your spouse want a fun way to reconnect by doing something out-of-the-ordinary, pretend to be tourists in your own town. Go online and download a list of the 50 top things to see and do in your city at www.citysearch.com. Or, buy a guidebook, check the entertainment section of your local newspaper, or head out to a restaurant or concert that was reviewed on the radio. Take a bike tour, see a concert, visit a museum, or check out a local landmark. Take pictures and buy souvenirs. You and your spouse will feel reinvigorated by your city and your time spent as a couple exploring a fascinating place — your home!

Be spontaneous with physical intimacy.

A crucial indicator of a happy marriage is a healthy sex life. Spontaneity will keep intimacy from becoming infrequent or predictable, whether you've been married 3 years or 30. Break out of your routine by changing your location or the time of day — if you always head to your bedroom, make love on the couch or in the kitchen; meet your spouse for a quickie over your lunch breaks. Explore a new position. Surprise your spouse during his or her morning shower. Switch roles; if you are usually the more aggressive one, allow your partner to be in control. Talk about your fantasies and commit to exploring them. Spontaneity promotes trying new things and keeps your relationship passionate and sexy.

Blow off your responsibilities, and don't overanalyze.

The world won't come to a screeching halt if you skip Pilates class, fail to mow the lawn, or don't get around to picking up your dry cleaning. Unhappy couples neglect each other for the sake of errands, chores, and other extracurricular activities. Happy ones know their priority is their partner, not their to-do list. So shirk your errands or play hooky from work and spend the time together. It doesn't matter if you plan a getaway or just spend the afternoon lounging in bed; just forget your worries and reconnect. Most important, don't allow yourself to feel irresponsible. Your world should revolve around your love, not the other way around.

Take it outside.

A change of scenery is sometimes all it takes to inject freshness back into a marriage — and it doesn't have to require a full-on vacation. Take your play outside. Suggest a jog, bike ride, or toss a football. Studies have proven that just a few minutes of natural sunshine a day boosts a person's intake of vitamin D, which improves mood, lowers blood pressure, and prevents bone loss. Additionally, fresh air promotes better breathing and circulation. Our busy lives often keep us cooped up in an office, car, or house for hours on end. Break the routine by having some spontaneous fun together while surrounded by Mother Nature.

Practice "planned spontaneity."

What can you do if spontaneity doesn't come naturally to you or your spouse? Practice the concept of "planned spontaneity." How it works: Write down all the important dates in your marriage (your spouse's birthday, your anniversary, holidays, etc.), then choose, at random, 12 more days (one day per month) for the coming year. Write down or set reminders in your planner or calendar for these dates. Not only will you never forget an anniversary, but you will be reminded once a month to send flowers or make a dinner reservation. Practicing "planned spontaneity" will most definitely keep your spouse guessing.

Chapter 9

Learning to Communicate

Communication is possibly the most crucial skill for a happy and healthy marriage. Effective communication allows a couple to resolve conflicts, avoid misunderstandings, and grow as a team. Communication helps create trust between two people. When you have an earnest discussion with your spouse, you learn to trust that he or she will respectfully listen without being judgemental, offensive, or defensive. In other words, happy couples create a safe environment in which to share their feelings, concerns, and issues.

Communication sounds easy enough; unfortunately, it is rarely that simple. Time and time again national surveys have found that communication problems rank consistently as a top factor that leads to divorce. Many times, a couple will think they are communicating effectively, but in actuality skip over the most important points, or eschew the most critical conversations. Even more frustrating, many struggling couples report feeling like they are talking about two completely different things when they argue. A wife might say her husband "isn't listening" or a husband might classify his wife as "argumentative." In fact, these problems may be a product of gender differences. Author Deborah Tannen's best-selling book You Just Don't Understand – Women and Men in Conversation has long claimed that gender differences in communication styles can lead to conflict if not addressed. Tannen notes that women tend to talk more than men at home. Furthermore, men tend to fall silent in conversation, while females tend to make noises that indicate they are listening. Women are also more inclined to express agreement and support, while men are more inclined to debate an issue.

So how do two very different types of communicators find common ground? The goal of communication is to say things in ways that your spouse can understand. It is crucial, at times, to stop and listen quietly. This will help you see things through your spouse's lens and hear the intended message. Most of all, couples must have patience with communication. Speaking the same language won't happen without commitment to changing the way you think and hear. The following simple principles will help you get started communicating effectively.

Be a reflective listener.

Reflective listening, or listening to what your spouse is saying rather than what you want to hear, is key to marital communication. What your spouse says and what you hear can be two radically different things. But individuals who practice reflective listening avoid needless misunderstanding and arguments. First, listen without interrupting. When your spouse finishes a thought, clarify by saying, "This is what I heard, is that what you meant?" Or repeat what you heard by asking, "Am I understanding you correctly that ...?" The simple act of asking for clarification or reflection can defuse a potentially tense situation and shows your spouse that what he or she says is valuable to you.

Be aware of your body language.

In a marriage, it is not always what you say, but how you say it that plays such an important role. Albert Mehrabian, a pioneer researcher of body language, found that a message is made up of about 7 percent verbal and 55 percent nonverbal communication. A furrowed brow can show doubt or skepticism. Touching your face can impart secretiveness. Hands rested on the hips can mean anger or frustration. Be it intentional or not, you don't necessarily want to send these kind of messages to your spouse. To avoid a misunderstanding, you and your partner should both aim to be aware of how you carry yourselves during a discussion.

Give verbal feedback.

Groundbreaking body language studies conducted in the 1950s concluded that 38 percent of what we perceive comes from tone of voice, inflection, and other sounds. Offering verbal feedback — such as saying "Mmm hmm," and "Uh huh" — is extremely important in marital communication, because it shows you are actively listening to your spouse. Deborah Tannen, author of You Just Don't Understand – Women and Men in Conversation, says that men have a tendency to stay silent during conversation, while women are more likely to give verbal cues. Too often, one partner feels like they are being tuned out during an important talk. Next time, nod and use verbal feedback.

64

Show respect, even if you disagree.

It is universally understood that you and your spouse will not see eye to eye at all times. How you both express yourselves, however, is crucial to a happy and healthy marriage. You must communicate your position with respect if you want your partner to listen to your side of an argument. If your tone becomes disrespectful, your spouse is likely to shut down and tune you out. Acknowledge that other opinions exist and are valid, even if you maintain your own point of view in the end. By staying respectful, even during a disagreement, you create communication built on trust. It has been said that the goal in marriage is not to think alike, but to think together.

Choose the right time to communicate.

One secret to communicating effectively with your spouse is to know when your partner is not in a place to be receptive to what you're saying. He or she may have had a stressful day at work or is feeling ill. If you approach your spouse for a discussion during an inopportune moment, he or she will not be fully receptive to you. Unsuccessful couples get frustrated or feel they are being brushed off; happy and healthy couples recognize when the timing is off and say instead, "Let me know another time that works better for you." Choosing the right time to communicate ensures that you and your partner will both be receptive to the message.

Learn to use "I" statements.

Nothing shuts communication down faster than when a person feels attacked. Watch how quickly your spouse stops wanting to communicate the instant you start a sentence with "You always ..." or "Why do you ... ." Instead, use "I statements" to express yourself, such as "I feel" or "I am thinking ... ." By using "I," you take ownership for your feelings. Instead of attacking another person, you are merely explaining how you feel. Consider the difference between saying, "You never take out the garbage because you don't care how this house looks," versus, "I feel embarrassed to have friends over when we have garbage piled up." Which sentence is more likely to produce positive results?

Avoid interrupting.

When healthy couples communicate, both people are given equal opportunity to speak. Interrupting is not only rude, but tells the person with whom you are speaking that you don't consider what he or she has to say to be important. When you interrupt, you tell your spouse your opinions are more valuable, that you are anticipating what he or she will say next, and that you don't respect your loved one enough to listen until he or she is finished speaking. Therefore, the next time you feel yourself jumping in before your spouse is done talking, bite your tongue. When your spouse pauses, ask, "Did you finish what you wanted to say?" Your spouse will be much more likely to let you say your piece if you allow him to say his.

Leave the past out of it.

Healthy couples live in the present. They work toward a happy future and do not dwell on past mistakes and troubles. Avoid drudging up old issues when you communicate with your partner — it merely creates resentment and keeps you both from moving forward. If you find you can't stop thinking about a past problem, devote a sole conversation to it. Try and resolve the problem in one fell swoop so it need not creep into future conversations. If a solution can't be reached immediately, agree to keep the issue out of present discussions. Learn from your mistakes as a couple but keep the past out of it to allow your marriage and partnership to continue to grow.

Never resort to threats or name-calling.

Healthy communication is built on a foundation of trust and love, which means never resorting to angry threats, name-calling, or other personal attacks. Inevitably, there will be times during your marriage when you feel furious and want to lash out. However, think before you speak, even when you are upset. Remember that insults cannot be taken back, and a word or nasty name that takes seconds to rattle off can stay in a marriage for years. The environment of trust you have created in your marriage is too important to damage with a careless comment. Strive to be the kind of couple whose love is too strong for threats and ugly names, even when you disagree.

Keep your cool.

Perhaps the most important thing you and your spouse can do to foster healthy communication is to stay calm during the course of an argument or heated discussion. Keep a level head, do not raise your voice, and stay positive throughout even the most difficult discussions. Keeping your cool is crucial to resolving issues, avoiding conflict, and maintaining closeness in your marriage. Marital experts often say it's not that a couple fights, but how they fight, that indicates whether their marriage will be successful. If you both keep cool, you will avoid screaming matches that damage your loving bond. Lastly, if one of you is unable to stay calm during discussions, consider seeing a counselor who can act as a mediator.

Chapter 10

Being Respectful

Having respect means working to understand your spouse's point of view because you believe it has value. Respect is shown by communicating without harsh tones or talking down to your spouse. Respect is shown by honoring your partner's wishes, even if you might not agree. Sound ideal? It is. Sound impossible to achieve? It's not!

Assess how respectful you are of your spouse. First, consider where your spouse ranks on your list of priorities. You may think you always place your spouse at the top, but your day-to-day reality might be very different. Do you work late often, placing your job above your marriage? Do you give in to your in-laws when you shouldn't, elevating your relatives above your spouse? Do you reprimand, criticize, or talk down to your spouse in public? If you answered yes to any of these questions, you are not giving your partner the respect he or she deserves.

Giving and receiving respect is a necessary for a marriage to work. Studies undertaken by the University of Washington have proven this to be true. In fact, researchers there have developed a tool that predicts with 87 percent accuracy which newly married couples will stay married and which will divorce within 4 to 6 years. The level of respect a person feels for their partner is a key ingredient of the formula. Sybil Carrère, lead author of the study, says, "The happiest couples are speaking almost in one voice because they are so tuned into each other's wants and desires. These people know the value of their partner in their life and know they are not out to get them. It is really beautiful music. With the unhappiest couples there is no symmetry. There is no respect for each other. Individuals are really nasty with each other and they struggle to find positive things to say about each other or the relationship."

To improve respect in your relationship, treat your partner with dignity, no matter the situation. Likewise, be the kind of person who commands respect, and your spouse will give it to you. These and the following simple principles will help you cultivate respect in your marriage.

Start by respecting yourself.

Albert Einstein once said, "Not until we respect ourselves can we gain the respect of others." In his day, Einstein was one of the most respected men on the planet, and continues to garner respect long after his time. Einstein was right about being unable to receive respect from others until you respect yourself. Experts agree that if you honor and value yourself, others will know you are worth being respected. For example, let's say your spouse snaps at you when he or she walks in the door after work. If you never address this behavior, you teach your spouse this behavior is acceptable. If you respectfully but assertively let your spouse know this behavior is not OK, you teach your spouse to treat you the way you feel you deserve to be treated: with respect.

Pay attention to your tone.

Your tone of voice is even more important to showing your spouse respect than what you actually say. The inflection and tonal frequency we add to our words imparts much about our mood and what we think about the person we're talking to. The next time you feel you are not coming across well to your spouse, make a point of listening to your tone of voice. Are you talking down to your spouse? Is your tone of voice insulting, belittling, or intimidating? Are you being sarcastic when your spouse is trying to be serious? When your spouse asks you to do something, do you respond with sincerity? Paying attention to your tone of voice ensures you will come across as genuine, loving, and respectful to your partner.

Respect your spouse's vulnerabilities.

You possess valuable information about your spouse that is probably unknown to most of his or her friends and other family. You know your partner's sensitive spots, peculiarities, and vulnerabilities. A respectful spouse never exploits these weaknesses in the course of an argument. For example, let's say you know that your husband is intimidated by his boss and avoids conflict at all costs. If you and your husband are arguing, it is disrespectful to say, "Now I see why you're so scared to stand up to your boss!" Stick only to the issue the two of you are facing. Never wield private or sensitive information in an argument, lest you risk disrespecting your spouse's feelings.

Avoid passive-aggressive behavior.

Being passive aggressive means expressing feelings or frustrations in underhanded ways instead of dealing with them outright (using stubbornness, procrastination, laziness, or any other indirect method). For example, instead of saying you are angry, you may "forget" to pick up dinner. Instead of admitting you are hurt, you may disappear for hours hoping it will provoke a reaction from your spouse. While passive aggression might work temporarily, it is not a long-term solution to your problem. Whatever is wrong will continue to be wrong until you face the problem head on. Put your issues on the table and have faith in your collective ability to solve a problem.

Respect your spouse's likes and dislikes.

You know the things your spouse likes, as well as what kinds of things get under his or her skin. Part of being respectful is making sure you avoid acting in ways you know your spouse doesn't appreciate. For instance, many people like some quiet time when they get home from work. If your spouse is one of these types, don't bombard him with questions and issues right when he walks through the door. You can also respect your wife's likes and dislikes by compromising with her on tasks she doesn't like. For example, if your wife hates doing dishes, agree that you will wash them if she will empty the dishwasher. Compromise is tied to respect because it shows you are equal partners.

Create a balance between your work life and home life.

Happy couples create a balance between work and home life. They avoid letting problems from work encroach on their relationship. You may have to stay late on occasion, but keep these instances to a minimum for the sake of your time together. And always make it home in time for dinner; the act of sitting down together for just 30 minutes each day helps families avoid drug abuse, smoking, and helps them reach higher levels of academic achievement, according to a 2006 report by Columbia University. If you have to, get in to work early so you can leave earlier to ensure you are home in time. Truly, there is no job more important than your marriage.

Respect if your partner needs alone time.

Even couples who are head-over-heels in love need time to themselves now and then. One or both of you may want time to yourself to read, take a walk, work out, paint, take a bubble bath, or indulge in another decompression activity. Alone time is a very personal preference — some people do not need or want any private time, while others need loads of it. Whatever the case in your marriage, respect your partner's preference. If your spouse asks for some alone time, don't take it personally or assume he or she doesn't want to spend time with you. A little space can go a long way in keeping both people de-stressed, relaxed, and happy.

Respect your loved one's hobbies and pastimes.

Show respect for what your partner enjoys, even if it's not a mutual interest. Maybe your husband lives for Monday Night Football, and you couldn't care less about the sport. Or maybe you can't understand why your wife would spend 2 hours every week at a book club meeting. Appreciate each other's interests by doing them together. Or, try to understand why your spouse enjoys the hobby. Unless your loved one's hobby infringes on your time together or makes you feel ignored (such as hours spent in front of a video game system or a "girls' night out" every weekend), you must respect each other's pastimes.

Respect your spouse's friends and family — even the tough ones.

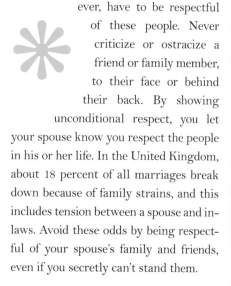

Just because you married someone you love doesn't mean you have to love his or her friends and family. You do, however, have to be respectful of these people. Never criticize or ostracize a friend or family member, to their face or behind their back. By showing unconditional respect, you let your spouse know you respect the people in his or her life. In the United Kingdom, about 18 percent of all marriages break down because of family strains, and this includes tension between a spouse and in-laws. Avoid these odds by being respectful of your spouse's family and friends, even if you secretly can't stand them.

Respect your partner's individuality.

When you stop trying to change your spouse, you have moved into a realm of respect. It is like you are saying, "You do not have to change to be loved and honored." Know that it may take years to reach this place. (Possibly after you have knocked your head against the wall in a series of unsuccessful attempts to provoke change.) Why is it so hard to give up wanting to change your spouse? Some marriage therapists believe that people find it easier to place the focus of frustration somewhere beside themselves. By trying to change their partner, they avoid looking inward at what needs to change about themselves. Bottom line: to fully respect your spouse, accept your partner, flaws and all.

Chapter 11

Learning to Compromise

Writer Leo Tolstoy, author of *War and Peace*, once said, "What counts in making a happy marriage is not so much how compatible you are, but how you deal with incompatibility." The union of two people who possess different opinions, likes, dislikes, and goals is not uncommon in a marriage; but in order for that marriage to work, the couple must be willing to compromise. Indeed, the act of compromise means giving up something you want in order to gain something even more important: peace and harmony in your relationship.

Compromise involves a give-and-take negotiation. By the end of the negotiation, neither side has received everything they want, but each party should have something satisfying. He wants Chinese food for dinner; she wants to go to her favorite Indian restaurant. In the end, they compromise on Italian, which they both like. This is a simplified example of a perfect compromise.

In real life, most compromises will be more complex. Couples in successful marriages note that regardless of the situation, a person must be willing to give more than they will receive. Indeed, marriage doesn't always mean giving 50 percent to meet in the middle. It means giving 100 percent and finding a solution you can both feel good about.

At times, you may struggle with deeper issues for which compromise may seem nearly impossible. These may include opinions on religion, politics, and parenting. In these cases, you must both work on acceptance. You may not be able to change your spouse, but you can always change your reaction.

Compromising is not a sign of weakness, but one of strength. It requires maturity, respect, and empathy. You have to be willing to let go of the scorecard and consider the greater good. You must be willing to change your viewpoint, or consider others. Finally, you must be open to giving more than you receive. Use the following principles to work toward compromise to create a happy, healthy environment in which your marriage can thrive.

Understand you are one half of a team.

Poet Phyllis McGinley once remarked, "Compromise, if not the spice of life, is its solidity. It is what makes nations great and marriages happy." With this in mind, realize that when you got married, you joined a team. You are one half of this team, and you must work to achieve your team's goals. Imagine a football team; if all the players run in different directions, chaos will ensue, and the team will never score a touchdown. Along the same lines, it is impossible to have a happy and healthy marriage if you and your partner constantly butt heads or pull each other in opposite directions. Once you stop viewing your issues as "me against you," solutions can be reached that will help your "team" achieve its goals.

Be collaborative in your compromise.

In 1989, a national survey published in American Demographics found that couples commonly compromised on just three issues: what to do on weekends, which restaurants to eat in, and where to travel on vacation. But by 1998, between 40 and 47 percent of couples said they compromised on topics as far ranging as spending or saving money, which TV program to watch, household expenses, the proper role of women, and career decisions. Since the 1990s, American couples have continued to turn to compromise to solve the majority of their problems. When you and your spouse collaborate to solve problems, you work as a team instead of fighting each another, which creates a healthy bond.

83

Don't compromise your own happiness.

Though fighting may exhaust you, don't give up if it means forsaking your own happiness. When no compromise is reached on an issue you care about, you will feel frustrated, haunted even, until it is resolved fairly. Giving in before you and your spouse are able to reach a compromise requires you to give up your happiness, which, with time, will cause you to resent your spouse. When faced with a problem, don't be afraid to stand your ground until a fair compromise is reached. Avoid dismissing the issue with statements like, "Fine, we'll do whatever you want." This sentiment is not what you really mean and will leave you feeling worse than if you had stuck around for a discussion that resulted in a compromise.

Show your partner you don't always have to win.

$\mathbf{A}$ difficult partner is someone who feels he or she must always win. There is no such thing as someone who is always a winner, however, so the person who thinks they are always right is very dangerous to the health of a marriage.

An important part of communication and compromise is the give-and-take nature of the negotiation process. If you always choose the movie or you make the majority of the decisions in your household, try working together with your spouse a bit more. Never think of compromise as winning or losing, simply as giving and taking to keep the peace in your partnership.

Share responsibilities around the house.

A major complaint in unhappy marriages is that household responsibilities are not shouldered by both partners. In fact, a study of second marriages, published in the Journal of Family Issues, noted that most people on their second marriage were more likely to share in household labor because they realize that the lack of balance contributed to the failure of their first marriage. Sharing household duties does not necessarily mean dividing them down the middle, some chores are better suited for one partner. The most important thing is that you and your spouse each take on household chores that complement your talents and time constraints, and that you both feel the arrangement is fair.

Determine your marriage's "no-compromise zones."

In some marriages, knowing when not to compromise is the glue that keeps two people from different cultures and backgrounds together. Indeed, it is normal for inherently different people to hold beliefs they cannot bend on — religion, political affiliation, abortion, and evolution are a few examples of issues that a person is usually unable to compromise on. Rather than forcing a compromise, recognize your marriage's "no-compromise zones." Your husband may support the death penalty and you may not, but if you can agree to disagree, you can avoid many unnecessary arguments.

Know when (and how) to let go.

One of the most important aspects of compromise is being able to let go when you recognize that you may not care as much about an issue as your partner. Consider whether something will really matter to you down the road. If you realize it doesn't, and you continue to push for your position, you are fighting just to win. People in successful marriages take the time to assess the importance of each issue and ask themselves, "How much will this matter to me in 5 days, 5 months, or 5 years?" For instance, if your husband insists on keeping an old armchair that you would have preferred to throw away years ago, remember that his happiness is more valuable in the long run than a silly chair. Learn to say, "It's not very important to me, so I'll just let it go."

Understand that it is normal to have recurring issues.

Are there certain topics or issues you and your spouse find yourselves going over again and again without finding a resolution? If so, you're not alone: One study published in the book The Marriage Clinic found that 69 percent of long-term couples experience perpetual problems that they have been dealing with for many years. Similarly, a separate study found that 47 percent of the things couples argue over are recurring issues — everything from finances to who gets the TV remote. Don't be discouraged by your recurring problems. Practice accepting your loved one's point of view and remember to stay calm and reasonable.

Learn the art of negotiation.

Being successful compromisers means you and your spouse must become great negotiators. First, take enough time to talk so you are not rushing. Pick a location that is quiet and peaceful. Eliminate distractions, like your cell phone. When you sit down together, build an atmosphere of trust. Look for common ground. Find places where you and your spouse can agree; these are places that are ripe for compromise. Seize opportunities to strike a deal. If things get a little heated, use a joke or neutral topic to alleviate tension. Acknowledge your emotions, but don't let them control you. Don't yield if an issue is very important to you. Lastly, remember that you are talking as teammates and a solution benefits you both.

Have empathy.

Compromise takes patience, commitment, and most important, empathy. Having empathy for your partner's position allows you to get in his or her head and walk in his or her shoes. Your ability to see where your spouse is coming from lets you make statements such as, "You have an interesting point of view" or "I understand why you feel that way." Being empathetic helps you respond to your spouse's opposing point of view in a kind, sincere, and respectful way. Finally, empathy helps you work toward a solution as a team. It allows you the ability to say, "I understand where you're coming from. Let's find an answer we're both comfortable with."

Chapter 12

Coping with Conflict

The German writer, Goethe, once said, "It is sometimes essential for a husband and a wife to quarrel — they get to know each other better." Indeed, some conflict is healthy for your marriage. In fact, a fascinating study by researchers at the University of Washington and the University of Wisconsin found that there are some types of fights that actually strengthen a couple's bond. These are fights in which partners feel free to be honestly angry with each other and get to make their point clearly and loudly. Co-author John Gottman believes that these fights help the relationship because they give the couple the strong sense that they can weather conflict together. According to Gottman, "Couples who have healthy fights develop a kind of marital efficacy that makes the marriage stronger as time goes on."

Indeed, conflict gives both people a chance to express their thoughts and feelings and shows you are both engaged in the relationship. In fact, marriages in which two partners do not fight are often deeply troubled; problems that are not confronted can grow and escalate and cause distance.

The keys to healthy conflict resolution include the three F's: flexibility, faith, and friendship. Flexibility helps you find solutions that work for both of you. A marriage that doesn't have flexibility will break. Secondly, faith helps you and your partner make it through rough spots: Marriage is not something you give up on when the going gets tough. Finally, friendship helps you and your partner feel less like enemies and more like buddies that need to find a way to work it out. Remembering that you and your spouse are friends helps to minimize angry outbursts, selfish demands, defensiveness, blaming, and criticism.

Learning to navigate your way through a conflict will result in a loving, happy home. Make a commitment to learning the simple principles that follow in this chapter, and use them every day.

Think before you speak.

At one point or another, you have probably been advised to think before you speak. Though it's one of the more common pieces of relationship advice, it is surprisingly hard to practice. When we get upset, our thoughts race and our reaction time lessens. It takes a genuine effort to slow your thoughts, become aware of them, and prevent the wrong ones from slipping out. Becoming aware can help you to stop yourself from saying something you might regret later. Research shows that couples who know how to self-edit while discussing highly charged topics — including parenting, finances, and in-laws — are more inclined to reach a point of compromise.

Recognize negative coping patterns.

Negative coping patterns are unhealthy behaviors or bad habits you perform repeatedly that serve to make a conflict worse. Some of these patterns include withdrawing, blaming, or acquiescing. Others include bullying or saying whatever you have to in order to get your way. Repeating these poor habits every time you and your spouse argue prevents you from getting anywhere new. By becoming aware of your patterns you can learn to break them and adopt new methods for resolving conflict. By recognizing your negative coping patterns, you can avoid exacerbating an already tense situation and move towards making real headway with your spouse.

Recognize what you are really fighting about.

Sometimes, arguments over small things are really an indication of larger issues that are not being properly addressed. Are you actually fighting over dirty dishes, or is there a deeper issue at hand? The real problem might be that you are resentful of your spouse spending extra hours at the office or that you need more help around the house. Other times, an argument may arise because one of you is on edge about a totally unrelated issue. Perhaps your wife is unhappy at work or your husband is stressed about bills. During a petty argument, recognize the underlying issues and say to your spouse, "Let's stop and address the real problem here."

Address behaviors, not personality traits.

If you argue with your spouse, do your best to address the troubling behavior instead of personality traits. For example, calling your spouse lazy is an attack on his or her character. Telling your spouse you are upset because he or she hasn't been helping with the housework is addressing a behavior that can be changed. If you criticize your spouse, he or she will get angry or withdraw. This is unfortunate, since your goal was to motivate the person to help out more. On the contrary, your spouse will be more likely to respond positively if you address the behavior and ask politely. In most cases, you are more likely to get cooperation if you do not personalize the problem.

Learn how your spouse cools off.

People tend to get overheated when they fight. An invaluable tool to a healthy marriage is learning how your spouse cools down and giving him or her the space to do so. Does your husband need an hour alone to calm down after a fight? Does your wife feel more relaxed and reasonable after she takes a brisk walk around the block? Some people find that their thoughts are much clearer after they sleep on it and return to the discussion in the morning. Once you recognize how your spouse cools off, allow him or her to do so; it will help you both resolve issues with the best possible attitude.

Don't go to bed angry.

You've surely heard of husbands or wives who choose to sleep on the couch after a big fight. But going to bed angry only means waking up to the same hurt feelings. A healthy issue is one that is dealt with openly and immediately, not overnight or over the course of several days. After an argument, resist the temptation to give your spouse the cold shoulder or withhold affection. Even though it may be difficult, lean over and give that kiss goodnight — you'll be amazed by how quickly this simple gesture melts away anger. By the next morning, you've likely regained your composure. The issue will probably still need work, but you'll find much of the animosity is gone.

Pick your battles.

Some issues are not worth arguing over, so don't do it. Picking your battles will keep you from fighting over petty, small things. But picking your battles is harder than it seems. It means evaluating how important a grievance is to you and assessing how willing you are to engage in an argument over it. People who don't know how to pick their battles come off as nagging or even harassing — they are seemingly upset with their partner every single day. Before you waste a fight, ask yourself, "Is this issue really worth arguing over?" "How much do I really care about this?" "Is anything positive going to come of this particular argument?" If you answer no to any of these questions, save your breath on the fight.

Fight fairly.

Arguing can be a healthy means of expressing your feelings, but shouting, name-calling, and criticism won't get you anywhere. In fact, 93 percent of couples who "fight dirty" will be divorced in 10 years, according to marital researchers at the University of Utah. This comes as little surprise; no one wants to be called "stupid" if they make a mistake, or be accused of being lazy or careless should they do something accidently that aggravates their partner. In the interest of saving your marriage, never resort to shouting or personally attacking your spouse. Fight fairly to ensure a happy and healthy relationship.

Argue in private.

Conflict can arise at any time — at a party, in the middle of a restaurant, even at the grocery store. Rather than hashing it out in public, save the argument for when you and your spouse are alone. Fighting in public, whether in front of friends or complete strangers, is detrimental to a healthy union and embarrassing for the people around you. Couples who argue in front of others alienate these people (and shouldn't be surprised when they stop being invited to parties and get-togethers). Furthermore, no one likes to be chastised or corrected in front of others. Although you may be fuming, wait until you are in private to continue the talk — it's respectful of both your marriage and the people around you.

Hold a state of the union.

Each January, the president addresses Congress and the nation in the State of the Union address, during which he discusses the health of the country, successes and achievements, and areas that need to be improved. But what about the state of your union? Every once in a while, sit down with your spouse and just talk about how things are going in your marriage. It doesn't have to be serious or official but use the time to check in on the status of your relationship. The more often you hold state of the unions, the quicker you will be able to spot snags before they grow into large problems. With each discussion, you and your partner will be able to proudly declare, "The state of our union is strong!"

Chapter 13

Practicing Forgiveness

Author Ruth Bell Graham once observed, "A good marriage is the union of two good forgivers." Indeed, forgiveness is one of the most crucial skills required if you and your spouse are to enjoy a happy, healthy marriage. Invariably, situations will arise where one of you will need to forgive or be forgiven. Practicing forgiveness strengthens your union and helps you foster trust, respect, fairness, and communication.

People often mistakenly believe that if they forgive someone who has harmed them, it signifies they are condoning an offensive behavior. But this is not so. Forgiving simply means you accept the reality of the situation and want to move forward to a more productive place in your relationship.

Additionally, forgiving is not necessarily something you do for the benefit of the person who has wronged you. Forgiveness is a process that is for your own personal benefit. Walking around with anger and resentment is extremely unhealthy; such a weight can completely drain a marriage.

Learning how to forgive is a way to lighten your load. When you forgive your spouse when he or she has hurt you, you release the resentment that came with the injustice. This does not mean that you must forget the event. It simply means you set yourself free from the negative feelings associated with the wrongdoing.

Although it takes a great deal of emotional work for you and your spouse to learn how to forgive, it is well worth it. Your mental, physical, and emotional health will improve when you no longer feel the need to hold on to fear, anger, and sadness. The following simple principles will teach you how to ask for and receive forgiveness in your marriage. As PhD Robert Karen writes, "True forgiveness isn't easy, but it transforms us significantly. To forgive is to love and to feel worthy of love. In that sense, it is always worthwhile."

Know that forgiveness is a process.

"Forgive and forget" is not as easy as it sounds. A Gallup poll that surveyed Americans on the topic of forgiveness found that 94 percent believed it is important to forgive, but a whopping 85 percent said forgiveness is something they are unable to do without help and work. First, you must acknowledge your feelings by letting the person know that he or she hurt your feelings. Second, tell the person who offended you that their words or actions were unacceptable. Then be prepared to accept an apology. Healing often feels like moving one step forward and taking two steps back. Do not rush any of these steps, and take solace in the fact that forgiveness is a difficult and slow process for anybody.

Admit responsibility.

Nothing will hinder the process of forgiveness like refusing to accept your part in an argument or indiscretion. Being humble enough to admit wrongdoing is a crucial step in healing. When your spouse tells you that you've hurt his or her feelings, listen intently. Fight the urge to become defensive. Don't get bogged down in the details of the event. Instead, focus on what you did or said that was hurtful or inappropriate. Take responsibility for your words and actions, be humble, and apologize. Admitting responsibility will also free you from guilt and shame, which are major obstacles to happiness in your marriage.

Offer a heartfelt apology.

Most relationships become stronger after an argument that ends with a heartfelt apology. For this reason, American poet Bryan H. McGill has noted, "There is no love without forgiveness, and there is no forgiveness without love." Both receiving and offering an apology can help reinstate lost confidence in your spouse. Strong marriages are built on a foundation of trust, which comes from knowing a person can take responsibility for themselves and also graciously accept flaws in others. Therefore, being open to accepting and offering a sincere apology will reinforce the bond between you and your loved one.

Give each other space.

Some of us need space to sort out our thoughts after a conflict, and even after receiving a sincere apology. You may be eager and ready to move on, but your spouse may need extra time to think and heal. Make it known that you are happy to give your partner some space should he or she need it and that you are willing to talk at any time. Allowing your spouse space for forgiveness lets healing occur naturally. As author Max de Pree once wrote, "We need to give each other the space to grow, to be ourselves, to exercise our diversity. We need to give each other space so that we may both give and receive such beautiful things as ideas, openness, dignity, joy, healing, and inclusion."

Let it all out, then let it go.

Part of the healing process of forgiveness involves venting to release hurt feelings. If you hold anger or sadness inside, it is likely to turn into bitterness or resentment. Toxic energy doesn't just go away, it festers inside a person. But you don't always need to vent to the person who hurt you. Vent in healthy ways. Pound a pillow; write a long, angry letter (you don't need to send it); yell in the shower; talk to a therapist, trusted friend, or even a pet. You'll find that after you've vented you are much less angry and may even be completely over whatever made you upset in the first place. For this reason, learning to vent is critical to moving forward and reaching a place of forgiveness.

Forgive completely.

So you say you have forgiven your wife for the time she got into a fender-bender in your car — but have you? The answer is "no" if you bring it up at every family event and use the topic as a weapon each time you have an argument. Once you decide to forgive, you must make a commitment to completely let go of the event, or else you haven't truly forgiven your partner. Instead of telling the car accident story every Thanksgiving, talk about the thoughtful gift your wife gave you for your birthday this year. Your wife will appreciate being let off the hook, and you will have successfully forgiven her.

Don't hang on to resentment.

Too many of us hang on to resentment and allow it to define who we are. Bottling up anger can have serious health consequences. Studies show that consistent, prolonged levels of anger, including resentment, make a person 5 times more likely to die before age 50. To make matters worse, resentful people tend to seek relief through dangerous habits, such as smoking and drinking, or through compulsive behavior such as workaholism and perfectionism. One secret to forgiveness is not to let wounds become your marriage's identity. Stop seeing yourself or your spouse as a victim and replace those thoughts with healthy and inspiring ones.

Know the difference between forgiving and accepting abuse.

Forgiving someone for abusing or mistreating you is not the same thing as accepting the behavior. Forgiveness is more about building a strong future that benefits from overcoming mistakes of the past. It was with this knowledge that Dutch physician Paul Boese remarked, "Forgiveness does not change the past, but it does enlarge the future." If someone in your life repeatedly makes the same mistakes, however, it is time to consider whether they are worthy of being forgiven. Do not let your ability to forgive be an invitation for someone to take advantage of you.

Forgive yourself.

Perhaps the most difficult person to forgive is yourself. Too often we are our own worst critics, our meanest enemies, our harshest judges. In fact, a University of Michigan study found that an incredible number of Americans — 44 percent of men and 43 percent of women — are unable to forgive themselves. However, the study also found that people able to forgive themselves are more satisfied with their lives and less likely to report symptoms of psychological distress, feelings of nervousness, restlessness, and sadness. While it is important to hold yourself to high standards, it is equally important to forgive yourself to move forward with a happier, healthier marriage.

Experience the freedom that forgiveness brings.

Theology professor Lewis B. Smedes has written, "To forgive is to set a prisoner free and discover that the prisoner was you." Indeed, forgiving is first and foremost a process about setting yourself free from anger, resentment, and guilt. Bearing these ugly feelings is extremely unhealthy, and can cause chronic health and emotional problems. Lighten your load by learning how to forgive. This does not mean that you must forget the event. It simply means you can set yourself free from negativity, resentment, and anger. Feeling free allows you and your spouse to experience the growth and happiness of successful marriages.

Chapter 14

Managing Household Responsibilities

Studies have shown that conflict over household chores and duties is second only to conflict over money in a marriage. This is mostly because in the 21st century, it is common for both spouses to work. In decades past, much of the household chores were a housewife's responsibility. But according to the Public Policy Institute of California, 54 percent of married women with a child under age 6 now participate in the labor market — double the amount who did so in the late 1960s.

With more women working outside of the home, there is more housework to be done and no one at home to do it. This has resulted in tension and stress for many married couples. Sometimes, women are expected to do the household chores on top of their full-time job, leaving them feeling resentful, haggard, and unfairly overworked. In other situations, no one does the chores, resulting in a frustrating and disorganized house. Both situations are recipes for marital disaster.

Dividing chores is a test of both respect and compromise. Statistics consistently show that despite attempts to share responsibilities around the house, one member of the family still takes care of the majority of the household tasks. If the division of labor is lopsided, problems will occur. Having a family and running a household as best done as a partnership. As Dr. Joyce Brothers has wisely said, "Marriage is not just spiritual communion, it is also about taking out the trash."

When responsibilities are divided, you and your spouse feel calm and in control. Small irritants are less likely to grow into bigger problems or set off needless quarrels and spats. Overall, maintaining a balance with household tasks will lower the stress in your union. Tackling chores as a team will promote balance and harmony and also get the job done twice as fast.

Apply the following principles to manage your family's household responsibilities and maintain a happy and efficient marriage.

Don't just ask for help.

Sixty-two percent of Americans say sharing household chores is very important for a happy and healthy marriage, according to a Pew Research Center study. When you approach your spouse about getting more involved around the house, do more than just ask. Merely asking for help around the house implies that chores are your job, and you're requesting additional assistance. On the contrary, these tasks are both you and your spouse's responsibility. Say something that reflects that, such as, "We need to divide the household chores in a way we both agree on." Then discuss how you can both share responsibility around the house, from washing dishes to picking up the children from soccer practice.

Discuss the chores you like, hate, and tolerate.

Before you divide your household chores, discuss with your spouse which chores you like, hate, and tolerate. You should be able to agree on a trade-off — for instance, you might decide that you'll be in charge of doing dishes because your spouse can't stand them, but he or she will empty the dishwasher, because that's your least favorite part. In fact, you might be surprised to learn that some people don't mind or even enjoy certain chores, such as vacuuming or folding laundry — they find them cathartic! No matter what you and your spouse's favorite or least favorite chores are, try to find ways to compromise on splitting them.

Make a master list of all family responsibilities.

Make a master list of all the tasks that keep your household running smoothly, such as cooking, cleaning, transportation, childcare, maintenance, and bill paying. Make a spreadsheet with categories for daily, weekly, monthly, and bimonthly chores, then divide the list among your family members. Hang the spreadsheet in a place where everyone in your family can see it, such as in the kitchen. Hold family members accountable to completing their chores. Provide some incentive by planning fun activities, outings, or even prizes for family members who complete their chores on time.

Understand that staying home is a full-time job.

In 2006, the Census Bureau reported there were 143,000 stay-at-home dads and 5.6 million stay-at-home moms in the United States. If one spouse stays at home, there is a tendency for the working spouse to regard all the housework as "not their job." However, know that being a homemaker — which involves cleaning, taking care of children, running errands, going to appointments, returning phone calls, and oodles of other time-consuming tasks — is not a vacation. The next time you come home from work and expect not to wash dishes, remember that taking care of a home is a full-time job in itself — so pitch in.

115

Avoid becoming a nag.

Equal division of household labor is very important to a marriage. A 2008 survey by the Pew Research Center found that couples rank it as more important to their happiness than having children. In fact, sharing chores outranked 6 of 10 issues couples normally associate with happy marriages. Given the importance of chores, it can be extremely frustrating if your spouse is not holding up his or her end of the bargain. But avoid nagging your spouse; it will only put him or her on the defensive, making the chances of changing the behavior slim. Simply remind your spouse that running a household involves partnership, just like your marriage. Also, remember to thank your spouse when he or she does chip in.

Make housework fun.

You may not love doing household chores, but you can make the time go faster by finding ways to make housework with your partner fun. Put on a favorite CD while you clean the kitchen; challenge each other to see who can sweep faster; toss your clothes into the hamper like basketballs. Set aside an hour or two out of your weekend to organize the house with your spouse, and make it as fun as possible. When you work as a pair, you might find that you start looking forward to that time together. Finally, reward yourselves for your hard work — enjoy an afternoon romp, a scoop of ice cream, or a fun night out together. As they say, "The couple that plays together, stays together."

Eliminate your expectation of perfection.

When doing laundry and taking out the trash, don't forget to also toss out your expectation of household perfection. Does it matter that the dishes aren't arranged perfectly in the dishwasher, or is it more important that your spouse made an effort to put the dishes away and didn't let them sit in the sink? Your spouse may need a bit of coaching, but avoid acting like a dictator. Sometimes, the effort is more important than a perfect result. If you insist on criticizing your spouse's every move, you may find yourself cleaning on your own. Eliminating the need for perfection will ensure that chores are happily shared.

Determine what the upcoming week holds, and make adjustments.

Being flexible is crucial to maintaining both a household and a marriage. There will be weeks when one of you is busy with special occasions, errands, or meetings. Before these times, be up front with your spouse about what your obligations are and how they will affect your ability to do your household chores. Alternatively, when your spouse comes to you with these concerns, be willing to make the adjustment to cover some of his or her duties. If your husband is going to have to put in extra hours at work, volunteer to make dinner. Think of what George Eliot meant when she wrote, "What do we live for, if it is not to make life less difficult for each other?"

See where you can cut back.

Take inventory of your list of chores. Are there changes you could make to your lifestyle that would save time, effort, and stress? For example, buying clothes that don't need to be dry cleaned will help you cut back on trips to the cleaners. Picking one day to devote solely to laundry prevents you from having to do it continuously throughout the week. Reevaluate time-consuming tasks. Are you grocery shopping four times a week? Look into having your groceries delivered. Assess whether certain chores need to be done as often as you've been doing them. Nothing terrible will happen if you mow the lawn every two weeks instead of every week. Consolidating tasks will make them more manageable.

Get outside help.

If you and your spouse are simply too busy for housework, examine whether your budget permits you to hire outside help. Hiring a cleaning person may be well worth it if it relieves a lot of stress from your marriage. If money is tight, look for bartering opportunities. Find friends and neighbors with similar needs. If you and a friend both have young children, alternate babysitting weekly. Or, offer to swap lawn mowing services with a neighbor. If you come across a home repair project that requires certain equipment or special skills, find a neighbor who is willing to help in exchange for your services at a later date. Getting outside help will lighten your load and alleviate a great deal of stress from your marriage.

Chapter 15

Nurturing Friendship in Your Partnership

Experts agree that a strong friendship is the foundation for a happy and healthy marriage. Much of the top research on marriage, conducted by Dr. John Gottman at the University of Washington, indicates that it is not whether a couple fights but rather the strengths that exist in the connection between them that determines the likelihood of their success. In other words, creating and sustaining friendship are the keys to a strong marriage.

Your friendship with your spouse is a living, growing thing, so keep it a priority. Spend time together. Make a commitment to staying friends, even during the rough patches. Stand by your spouse when the outside world is hard or painful. Talk often and get to know each other well; it doesn't always have to be profound, just connect. Studies show that couples who build a strong foundation of friendship are better able to anticipate and resolve conflict, enjoy a more satisfying sex life, and are better equipped to make the transition into parenthood.

You can nurture the friendship in your marriage on a daily basis through small but meaningful gestures. Get up 20 minutes early to enjoy breakfast together before leaving for work. Call to say hello to your partner during the day. Do something thoughtful and unexpected, such as bringing home take-out from your spouse's favorite restaurant. Anticipate your spouse's needs, including taking over certain errands when your spouse is having a stressful week. Make time to do things together, like going for a jog or watching a favorite TV show. These small moments of friendship go a long way in preventing and dealing with times of strife.

Philosopher Friedrich Nietzsche wrote, "The best friend will probably get the best wife, because a good marriage is based on talent for friendship." With this in mind, commit to nurturing your friendship for a happy, healthy marriage. Use the following simple principles to learn the secrets to cultivating the friendship in your marriage over the years.

Treat your spouse like a friend.

With marriage comes the promise of unconditional love and friendship. Successful couples treat each other like treasured friends; unsuccessful couples often treat each other worse than they would a friend or even a stranger. Being polite is not something reserved for use outside of your home. Don't take for granted the fact that your spouse has pledged to always be there for you. Lifetime love is a gift to be cherished. Acting petty or mean just because you can get away with it is unacceptable and a recipe for disaster. Treat your spouse as well and even better than you do your friends and acquaintances — always be respectful, thoughtful, supportive, and kind.

Always put your spouse first.

Putting your spouse first means giving without considering what you might get in return. When you view your marriage as a team, this becomes easy because placing your spouse's wants and needs above your own serves the common good of your partnership. Putting your spouse first can be as simple as agreeing to see the movie your spouse suggests or staying home from a social event because your spouse isn't feeling well. When both people give unselfishly, friendship and trust are cultivated.

123

Learn all there is to know about your loved one.

Do you know your spouse's biggest dreams and deepest fears? What is your spouse's favorite meal, bottle of wine, or movie genre? Do you know her career goals for the next 10 years? What about his idea of a perfect vacation? A surprising number of partners know less about their spouse than their friends. This is because spouses don't always have the kinds of conversations that lead to learning these details. Nurturing your marital friendship means educating yourself on your spouse's likes and dislikes, as well recognizing how the person has grown and changed over the years in those respects.

Be your spouse's rock.

Philosopher Albert Camus wrote, "In the depth of winter, I finally learned that within me there lay an invincible summer." Your marriage will have summers and winters — good times and bad — and you must find solidarity with your partner if you are to weather both seasons. These difficult times will eventually pass, but until they do, they will test your friendship on a daily basis. Be prepared to be a good friend to your spouse during tough situations, such as unemployment, depression, sickness, or stress. Often times, this solidarity is the only thing that gets a couple through a difficult time.

Be a soft place to land when your spouse is struggling.

In happy and healthy marriages, both people act as safe havens for their partner. When your spouse has a bad day or is struggling with a difficult issue, be a soft place to land. Don't feel you must offer advice when your spouse is down. Many times, it is more helpful to be a friend who listens quietly. Be a shoulder to cry on after a loss. Suspend all judgement and concentrate on helping your spouse rest, relax, and rejuvenate. Simply act as a presence that is comforting and secure. Be sure that your spouse knows that if he or she trips and falls, you will provide a soft place to land.

Be a cheerleader for your partner.

Forming a strong friendship with your spouse means being his or her biggest supporter. So cheer your loved one on to success, be it securing a promotion, cultivating a hobby, or achieving a life-long dream. Being a cheerleader for your spouse means lending your support wherever necessary and making the person feel like he or she can never fall short of greatness. Celebrate your partner's victories, big and small. Your enthusiasm shows that you understand and embrace your partner's goals and dreams, and support them as if they were your own.

Keep each other's secrets.

When a couple goes through life together, they end up sharing confidential and sensitive information about one another, including secrets, fears, and past mistakes. Nurturing your friendship means being a quiet ear to listen, but also guarding those secrets closely. Be careful to never reveal your spouse's fears or secrets to friends or family members, even when you are upset. Friendship in your marriage relies heavily on trust and integrity, so keep private information that way and you will understand what poet W.B. Yeats meant when he wrote, "I have spread my dreams beneath your feet; tread softly because you tread on my dreams."

Make yourself completely available for at least 15 minutes a day.

If you are like most Americans, your day is filled with work, errands, household chores, childcare, exercise, cooking, and many other commitments. However, none is more important than your commitment to your best friend: your spouse. Make yourself 100 percent available to your partner for at least 15 minutes a day. Talk to each other about your day, go for a walk, or simply snuggle up on the couch. Being completely available means eliminating distractions such as email, cell phones, television and paperwork. Fifteen minutes may not seem like a lot, but that time to download with your partner is extremely valuable to your marital friendship.

Reach out after a fight.

Lovers and best friends will always have disagreements, but how you make up after a fight is crucial to the success of your marriage. Unhappy couples will often reject each other and pull away after they have an argument. Instead, reach out to your spouse after a fight, even though your gut feeling may be to distance yourself. Don't flee the scene of the fight by leaving the house.

Also, keep the lines of communication open by never resorting to the silent treatment. Although it is normal to feel vulnerable after a fight, don't wait for your partner to initiate an apology. Reach out to him or her with humor, affection, and sincerity.

130

Give your spouse the benefit of the doubt.

Actor Michael J. Fox once explained that the key to his marriage is that he and his wife always give each other the benefit of the doubt. As someone who suffers from Parkinson's disease, Fox knows about the benefits of having a spouse whom you can count as a good friend when the chips are down. Giving your spouse the benefit of the doubt means that you know you both will make mistakes from time to time, but you trust in the strength and good nature of your bond. By relying on trust, gratitude, and friendship, your spouse is more likely to live up to your expectations.

Chapter 16

Fostering a Healthy Social Life

Happy and healthy married couples cultivate active social lives as a pair, as well as encourage their partners to nurture independent friendships. Not only is having great friends a lot of fun, but studies have consistently demonstrated the health benefits of close friendships. Reliable friendships are a natural stress-reducer, can lengthen your lifespan, and can reduce the incidence of depression and insomnia.

And, just as solidarity with your mate will help you weather the tough times, having a strong, supportive network of friends will help you both when you are struggling. It is critical to have a close friend who you can talk to, other than your spouse. There will be times when you need a totally sympathetic ear to listen or a shoulder to cry on — and that is where your social circle comes in.

Additionally, an active social life keeps you growing as a couple. Friends can help you and your spouse discover new interests and passions you might not have considered otherwise. Both single friends and other married couples can recommend or introduce you to new activities, clubs, and restaurants. Remember that openness, flexibility, and a sense of adventure are keys to having a healthy social life as a couple.

Having an active social life can help you and your spouse live longer, healthier and happier lives, so work on fostering a strong, supportive network today. Think of your social time as your opportunity to relax, regroup, and renew. Encourage one another to have fun. When you see how relaxed and happy you both feel after a fun social event, you will understand why French writer Marcel Proust said, "Let us be grateful to people who make us happy, they are the charming gardeners who make our souls blossom."

Use the principles in this chapter to learn how to spend time together, and also to nurture your independent friendships. You and your spouse will reap the health benefits of having a healthy social life.

Nurture commonalities.

The first step to creating a healthy social life is finding commonalties between you and your partner. Marriages suffer when a wife must drag her husband to the opera or a husband forces his wife to accompany him to a work party where she knows no one. Although it is expected that your spouse will go with you to these types of events now and then, they should not form the basis of your social life. A healthy marital social life is one that is fun, rewarding, comfortable, and invigorating for both people. Make a list of activities that you and your spouse both enjoy, and nurture those commonalities — for instance, if you both like the water, consider getting SCUBA certified together. Cultivate your social life with common interests.

Be creative.

Openness, flexibility, and creativity are keys to a healthy marital social life. Start by turning off the television; watching a sitcom or movie can be relaxing, but it won't help you and your partner creatively enjoy one another. Instead of sedentary activities like watching TV, choose hands-on activities that will expand your cultural horizons or help you find new creative interests. Consider volunteering, taking cooking classes, joining a political organization, attending wine-tasting events, getting a membership at a museum, joining an improv comedy group, signing up for art classes — even karaoke counts as a creative endeavor. No matter the event, the important thing is that you and your partner do it together.

133

Be adventurous.

Setting off on an outdoor adventure will give you and your spouse more confidence, help you get physically fit, and introduce you to other active couples. In addition, getting outside your comfort zone will strengthen your bond as a pair. Think of all the exciting stories you'll have to tell! Sit down with your spouse and agree on adventurous physical activities you can try together. Some ideas include skydiving, skiing, horseback riding, snorkeling, yoga, traveling internationally, or playing on a co-ed softball team. As civil rights activist Dr. Harold Thurman said, "Don't ask what the world needs, ask yourself what makes you come alive and then go and do that, because what the world needs is people who have come alive!"

Be aware of your spouse's social style.

Popular advice columnist Ann Landers once said, "At every party there are two kinds of people — those who want to go home and those who don't. The trouble is, they are usually married to each other." Your wife may be someone who loves to play team sports but hates to watch them. Your husband may enjoy attending big parties but hates to dance. Your wife may relate better at small, intimate gatherings but feels uncomfortable if there is drinking involved. Get to know what makes your spouse feel comfortable in social settings. You may never be able to change a person's social style, so it is better to choose social settings that satisfy you both.

Eliminate toxic social scenes or people.

Just as chemicals are toxic to your body, certain people or social scenes are toxic to your marriage. Is there someone in your social circle that makes you feel uneasy? Do you have a friend who brings out the worst in you? You may have to step away from those friendships. Perhaps you find that hanging out with a particular circle of single friends places you in situations your spouse would disapprove of. If so, it might be time to find a new social circle. Only you can determine what social scenes are healthy for your relationship. Ask yourself, "Is this person or situation contributing to my well-being?" "Would my spouse be happy if he or she was here?" If not, remove yourself from those situations.

Find other couples with healthy social attitudes.

Just as you should identify people and social scenes that are toxic to your marriage, it is equally important to identify friends who are healthy for your marital social life. A recent study linked positive, nurturing friendships with healthier exercise, diet, and sleeping habits. (And whose relationship didn't improve when their partner ate well and got more sleep?) Gravitate toward couples with similar values, goals, and interests. They should also have positive attitudes about marriage and family life. These friends should make you and your partner feel like you belong in the group.

Have a regular "couples' night."

The Centers for Disease Control and Prevention reports that married adults have lower rates of heart failure, cancer and other diseases, and develop tighter networks of emotional support than those who are divorced, widowed, or never married. Now that you've identified other couples who share your interests and values, enrich your relationships with them by scheduling a "couples' night." Once a month, gather with your married friends and be social. Take turns going to one another's homes. Barbecue, play board games, have a wine and cheese party, or just sit around and chat. You'll have fun, strengthen your social network, and do something good for your health.

Encourage a girls' or guys' night out.

The time you spend together as a couple is crucial, but you also need time to nurture independent friendships. Good friendships keep you and your spouse emotionally and physically healthy. They also allow you to participate in activities your spouse doesn't necessarily enjoy. In this spirit, allow your spouse to have a boys' or girls' night out from time to time. It will benefit your marriage if your husband plays golf with the guys or if your wife goes out to dinner and drinks with her girlfriends. Encourage one another to have fun within your independent friendships. Your spouse will be happier with a strong support network; plus, he or she will likely return to you feeling relaxed and renewed.

Be conscious of your public behavior.

Fostering a healthy social life as a married couple includes evaluating your behavior as individuals and addressing possible issues. Ask yourselves: "Are we participating in any unhealthy or provocative behaviors?" For example, do you flirt with the waiter or waitress at restaurants? Do you drink too much, causing your spouse embarrassment? Do you get loud or angry during sporting events? Inappropriate public behavior can be very uncomfortable for a spouse and, thus, highly damaging to a marriage. Your actions reflect on your partner, so be honest about dangerous, rude, or embarrassing social conduct. The next step is working with the help of a professional to change inappropriate behavior.

Grow your social circle.

In 2005, a groundbreaking research study published in the Journal of Epidemiology and Community Health found that having a network of good friends can extend a person's lifespan. Studies show that women are far more likely than men to make friends. In 2004, life expectancy for American women was 5.2 years longer than men and many scientists suspect their adeptness at making and retaining friends explains why. To extend your life and your partner's, incorporate new and interesting people into your social circle. It will benefit your health, attitude, and emotional well-being. The tough times will always be easier with the support of good friends.

Chapter 17

Loving Your In-Laws

In-laws can be a source of love and support. Many times, however, they are a source of marital strife. We've all heard the jokes — as Mark Twain once wrote, "Adam was the luckiest man; he had no mother-in-law." Indeed, it can be a feat to get along with your in-laws if you experience cultural, educational, generational, religious, and moral differences. You may have chosen your spouse, but the truth is that you cannot, and probably wouldn't, choose your in-laws. To avoid a tug-of-war between relatives and spouse, you must create workable, appropriate boundaries for the relationship. By respecting the needs of both parties, you can create a bridge between your past and future.

There are many reasons to strive for a healthy relationship with your in-laws. This extended family can give you much-needed help with finances or childcare. Furthermore, a healthy relationship with your in-laws also shows respect for your spouse and his or her roots. You and your partner both have histories that should be respected in your home.

For better or for worse, your marriage comes with a new set of family members who are here to stay. You will quickly recognize that every family has different traditions and ways of doing things. While you should always put your marriage first, it is important to respect these different traditions and honor at least a few of them. Likewise, it is respectful to carve out a space in your home life for your in-laws. When they are visiting, truly treat them as family.

Rather than feeling stressed or strained each time the in-laws come to visit, use the simple principles in this chapter to create happy relationships with your immediate and extended family. You will find it is relatively easy to keep the peace and even form strong bonds. Every couple wants to live in harmony with their family. The following principles will help protect your marriage while creating a healthy bond with your extended family.

Make it known that your spouse comes first.

At times you may feel as if you are stuck in the middle of a tug-of-war between your spouse and your parents or in-laws. Both parties may be vying for your attention, affection, or loyalty. Make it known, gently and respectfully, that your spouse and immediate family are your priority.

You and your spouse need to establish your own family traditions, lifestyle, and values. Your in-laws must respect that. By giving your marriage priority, you choose your new role — the adult spouse — over your old role — the child. Make sure your partner comes first, and make sure it is clear through your words and actions.

Respect your in-laws, no matter what.

It is imperative that you treat your in-laws with respect at all times, even if they are not always courteous to you. While it may be difficult to take the higher road when someone is critical of you, you don't want to give your in-laws reasons to dislike you. Take a few deep breaths or leave the room — whatever it takes to stay calm. Avoid escalating the problem. Showing respect, no matter the situation, is a way of letting others know how you would like to be treated. It is also a good example to set for your children and a signal that you are open to finding common ground. If nothing else, respecting your in-laws means honoring your spouse, and he or she will appreciate your efforts on behalf of the family.

Set boundaries.

Setting boundaries is a key survival skill for dealing with extended family. Before your in-laws visit, sit down with your spouse and define boundaries for visits, time with grandchildren, holidays, and your marital privacy. For instance, it is not appropriate for your in-laws to show up at your home unannounced. Insist that they call first so they don't intrude on private family time. Or, perhaps your mother-in-law constantly offers unsolicited parenting advice. Make it clear that you respect her feelings, and you will incorporate her ideas where you see fit, but you have your own ways of doing things. Be assertive but gentle, and your in-laws will respect the boundaries you and your spouse have set.

Establish a firm set of ground rules for your home.

When you create a firm set of ground rules and make them clear to your in-laws, you and your spouse take an important step toward avoiding conflict. For example, you might conclude that 5 days is the limit to how long in-laws may stay in your house. Let family know what you expect of them when they visit; make it clear that you would like everyone to make their own bed each morning, or to rinse their dishes. You might ask your in-laws not to bring candy for your children when they visit. Explain that, while you appreciate the thoughtful gesture, you have a no-sweets policy. With a firm set of rules, you will nip many problems in the bud.

Avoid criticizing your in-laws to your spouse.

Your spouse will naturally have some loyalty to his or her family, so avoid criticizing them. If you need to vent, choose a trusted friend, not your spouse. Don't make your in-laws the butt of jokes. Avoid picking on every little comment or misstep they make. Being critical of your in-laws will only make your spouse defensive and create tension between the two of you. On the occasion that an in-law steps over the line, bring the issue to your spouse respectfully and without attacking the person who wronged you. You might say, "Something your father said really confused me." Because you've chosen to put each other first, your spouse will be receptive to your concern.

Never involve your in-laws in your marital issues.

Protect your marital privacy by never involving your in-laws in your marriage's private issues. Let your extended family know only what you choose to tell them. If you don't want unsolicited advice on your marriage, don't invite it by sharing your latest disagreement or fight with your in-laws. If you bad-mouth your spouse to your parents or in-laws, you are inviting your extended family to choose sides. When you share your anger or frustration, your in-laws will focus on that, not on when you and your spouse make up. If your in-laws ask how things are going in your relationship, simply smile and say, "Just great, thank you."

Build bridges wherever possible.

Foster your relationship with your in-laws independent of the one you have through your spouse. When you build bridges with your in-laws, they become more inclined to support you and treat you like family. You may even discover you have things in common. Show interest in their interests — share favorite foods, pastimes, and hobbies. Talk to them about their heritage and where their family comes from. Do something fun — go to a local event or a funny movie. Cultivate happy memories together. Email your mother-in-law biweekly or monthly, even if it's just a brief hello to say you're thinking of her. Make it known you are reaching out and, hopefully, they will reach out to you.

Respect differences in culture and upbringing.

Regardless of your in-laws' ethnicity, country of origin, or religious beliefs, you will most definitely encounter differences between your upbringing and cultural values and those of your extended family. The key to loving your in-laws is being open-minded and accepting. Based on their background, they may have very different ideas about child-rearing, religion, the role of the man in the family, tradition, holidays, and more. Show interest in your in-laws' background and beliefs, but also invite them to learn more about your culture and values. Understanding breeds acceptance, which allows you to create new family rituals.

Make your in-laws feel included.

When in-laws feel neglected or distanced from the family, they tend to act out. Since you've already set boundaries and guidelines, you should be able to ward off overbearing behavior. However, you still want to include them whenever possible. Call right away when you have family news to share. Send holiday cards with updates on you and your children. Invite them to important family events, including graduations, sports games, award ceremonies, and birthdays. If you spend a holiday with one set of in-laws one year, make it a point to visit the other set the next year. Inviting them into your life will prevent them from feeling left out and enable you to preserve the boundaries you've established.

150

Understand that you can't change your in-laws, only your reaction.

You have probably heard the saying, "Grant me the serenity to accept the things I cannot change." You may not be able to change the way your in-laws treat you, but you always have control over your own reaction to them. Perhaps, despite your best attempts, your in-laws continue to be aloof, rude, bossy, or nosey. Commit yourself to letting their words and actions roll off your back, without allowing your mood or attitude to turn negative. You and your spouse can cope with the problem by maintaining a unified front and agreeing not to react to whatever negativity they throw at you.

Chapter 18

Strengthening Your Sense of Family

There is nothing more rewarding than being surrounded by the warmth of a loving family. Creating this environment begins with a happy, healthy relationship between you and your spouse. Having a strong sense of family contributes to the satisfaction in your marriage, as well as to the well-being of your community. As marriage expert Diane Sollee of smartmarriages.com says, "They say it takes a village to raise a child. That may be the case, but the truth is that it takes a lot of solid, stable marriages to create a village."

The decision to have children can impact a marriage tremendously, and not always for the better. In fact, 70 percent of wives report feeling a decrease in their marital satisfaction during the first year after having a baby. Children can add emotional, physical, and financial strain to a couple's already hectic life. So how can you be sure you experience the joyful side? Noted marriage researcher Dr. John Gottman believes the key is to establish a rock-solid union before welcoming additions to your family. "Focus on your marital friendship," he stresses. A couple with an already strong sense of family will be better prepared for the transition into parenthood. Likewise, as they grow, your children will experience the sense of belonging that makes for healthy, successful individuals. It has been proven that children raised in affectionate, loving households go on to do well in school and stay away from dangerous behaviors like drinking and drug use.

Dr. Gottman urges married couples to develop and maintain their "we-ness" as they build a family. This means never abandoning your playful intimacy with one another. If you have children, it will help them to see you being affectionate. Don't worry about being perfect parents. It's okay to show your children that you make mistakes, as long as you work as a team to compromise and problem-solve.

Whether or not you have children, use the following principles to create an identity for your family and strengthen your sense of togetherness.

Make memories as a family.

To avoid getting caught up in the humdrum of daily life, make it a priority to create special memories with your family. Getting outside is a quick and easy way to lighten everyone's mood and share an experience that is both entertaining and healthy. Visit a water park or go to the zoo. Vacationing is another great way to make memories. Think of a special place or landmark you would like to see; make sure you include your whole family in the planning process. Whether you spend the day at Disneyland or take a road trip to the Grand Canyon, realize that it doesn't really matter where you go — just that you are all on a journey together.

Eat dinner together.

It has been proven that families who eat meals together have closer relationships and raise more successful children. In fact, the National Center on Addiction and Substance Abuse found that children who eat regular meals with their families have less stress, eat better, get better grades in school, and are less likely to use alcohol and drugs. Also, enjoying a TV-free meal together can help your family eat better. A study published in the Journal of the American Dietetic Association suggests that families who eat dinner together with the television off eat more fruits and vegetables than those who eat separately or with the television on. So, get together nightly for dinner to strengthen your sense of family, and your health.

Create family traditions.

It is important for your family to create rituals and traditions. Though it is easy to abandon traditions as your children get older, such rituals are critical to their development and to your identity as a family and as a couple. Don't let your busy schedules prevent you from making memories; these traditions will cement your family's bond for a lifetime. So make Tuesday movie night; make Wednesday night take-out night. Go to your favorite pizzeria on Friday. Take a hike every Saturday, and read a story before bed a few times a week. Take an annual ski trip. Get together with the same relatives every Thanksgiving Day. Do whatever it takes to keep your family close with daily, weekly, and yearly traditions.

Give back to your community as a family.

Creating a strong sense of family also means contributing positively to your community. By getting the whole family to volunteer, you can strengthen your bond while helping others in need. Volunteer at a homeless shelter, write letters to soldiers, pick up trash around your neighborhood, help out at the Humane Society, or adopt a less-fortunate family during the holidays. Serving your community will teach your children that they have a purpose larger than themselves, and help them feel grateful for everything they have. Give your family a common responsibility, and it will help you unite as a group.

Get to know the important people in your family members' lives.

For a strong sense of family, be active in the lives of your family members. This means getting to know the people that are important to your spouse and children. If your spouse is especially close to a coworker you don't know well, invite that person to dinner. Make an extra effort to get to know your spouse's close friends. Get acquainted with the kids who are influencing your children. If they have friends who respect and share their values, it will help protect them from peer pressure. Plan activities with your kids and their friends — take them all bowling or ice skating. Getting to know the people in your family members' lives will build trust and camaraderie.

Get a family pet.

Studies have shown that people who have regular interaction with pets are happier and healthier. The Centers for Disease Control reports that having pets can lower your blood pressure, cholesterol, and reduce feelings of loneliness by increasing opportunities for exercise, outdoor activities, and socialization. Having a family pet also promotes bonding and a sense of responsibility. Children will benefit as they turn to pets when they need a friend, confidante, or protector. In a national opinion poll conducted in the U.K., pets were reported to be nearly as important as parents and grandparents in a small child's life. If you don't already have a family pet, consider getting one.

Big Idea

157

Create a balance between work and family.

In 2003, the unanimous passage of the U.S. Senate's National Work-Life Initiative allowed October to be declared National Work and Family Month. The Senate agreed that "reducing the conflict between work and family life should be a national priority." It is likely that you and your spouse are part of the 85 percent of U.S. workers who have immediate, day-to-day family responsibilities outside of their jobs. Start by talking to your boss about the possibility of working from home or working a compressed schedule. Most important, put family rituals and needs first. Chat over dinner, help with homework, attend your child's events, or enjoy a family outing.

Create and share your family's legacy.

American humorist Erma Bombeck once said, "Now is the time to enjoy our lives, enjoy the lives of those who have gone before us, and the lives of those who we have helped to bring us into this world. Write your stories, read your stories, enjoy who you are." In this spirit, draw a family tree, tell your children about your family's history and countries of origin, and share pictures of grandparents. Create the legacy of you and your spouse as well — talk about how you met, your first date, and your wedding day. Make scrapbooks of your children's lives. Encourage them to write their own memoirs. It is important to your family, as well as for the generations to come, to create and share your legacy.

Be mindful of how you and your spouse interact.

As a healthy couple, always be conscious of how you interact in front of your children. Your children are like sponges, soaking up every word and action. If there is tension or anger between you and your spouse, they will feel it. Never criticize or name-call; it will give the impression that it is appropriate to speak to others that way. Your children do not have to believe that you and your spouse never fight, just that you can do so with civility and respect, and that arguments never threaten the love in your household. After a fight, make sure to talk to your kids about how you resolved the issue and remind them that you love each other (and them) very much.

Know that the best gift you can give your family is a healthy marriage.

You and your spouse need not worry about being perfect parents. You are human, with flaws. It is normal to disagree, argue, and make mistakes. You will not be able to be at every soccer game or Boy Scout meeting. You will not always know what to say when someone cries. You can, however, commit to keeping your family connected with honesty, respect, and communication, and by practicing the principles in this chapter. Finally, the best thing you can offer your family is a healthy marriage. As motivational speaker Naomi Rhode says, "We can't all leave a prestigious background or lots of money to our children, but we can leave them a legacy of love."

Chapter 19

Enriching Your Sex Life

Sex is one of the most important aspects of a happy and healthy marriage. More than an expression of your deepest love, having sex with your mate can improve all areas of your life. The health benefits of sex include a reduced risk of cancer, disease, heart attack, and stroke. Having sex gives you confidence, relaxes you, clears your mind, improves your ability to focus, and even reduces depression. So why is it that so many American couples feel embarrassed, nervous, or flat-out afraid to talk about sex?

Your sex life can be a touchy subject, often because it serves as a barometer for the health of a relationship. Couples in trouble may not want to acknowledge that their private, intimate life is suffering. Truly, sex can bring you closer together, or drive you apart. The key to a wonderful sex life begins, like so many things, with communication. Your partner is your trusted friend and confidante. Despite this, many of us feel afraid to talk about what our sex life needs — what is wonderful and what it might be missing.

The University of Chicago's National Opinion Research Center Adults reports that, on average, Americans have sex about 61 times per year, or slightly more than once a week. Between our careers, children, social lives, and financial responsibilities, finding time for sex and intimacy can be a real challenge. Likewise, sexual frequency decreases as we age. So, how can you keep the passion that first brought you together alive?

First, view sex as more than just "the act." Remember that sex provides mutual pleasure, shows meaningful physical and emotional closeness, and is a way to show your partner you are in tune with his or her needs.

Having a sex life that meets both partner's needs is vital to your happiness as a couple, so make room for intimacy. The following principles will help you and your spouse enjoy a satisfying sex life as part of a happy and healthy marriage.

Don't be afraid to talk about sex.

Talking openly about sex with your spouse is one way to enrich your sex life and keep it passionate. Discussing your wants, needs, desires, and sexual fantasies can be enlightening, liberating, and a serious turn-on. Of course, it can also be intimidating to talk about sex. When you and your spouse share, keep in mind that you are also best friends. View your marriage as a sanctuary of trust, one in which you don't have to be afraid to talk openly and honestly. Be sensitive to each other's feelings, but don't hold back. You're not discussing what is lacking, only what you might gain together. Be willing to listen and share, and you will reap the rewards of a passionate sex life.

Address issues that may be following you to bed.

If you are having trouble connecting sexually with your spouse, think about what emotional issues are lurking beneath the surface of your relationship. Sometimes problems in bed have nothing to do with sex. Unresolved conflict or unexpressed anger can hinder feelings of love and closeness necessary for a happy sex life. If you carry around negative feelings for your partner, you will inevitably find yourself less attracted to him or her. Don't allow your issues to fester; take time to talk about what's really going on. Clearing things up emotionally will allow you to reconnect physically.

Acknowledge gender differences in sex.

Research has shown that men and women view sex very differently. If you feel like you and your spouse aren't on the same page sexually, you may need to take gender differences into account. Men are turned on by visual cues and often view sex as the main route to connect with their wives. Women, on the other hand, need to be aroused physically or psychologically and are driven by a desire for emotional connection. They will respond to subtler cues, such as an affectionate touch, romantic meal, or even an intimate conversation. Romance novelist Barbara Cartland was right when she said, "Among men, sex sometimes results in intimacy; among women, intimacy sometimes results in sex."

Exercise for a more satisfying sex life.

Countless studies have shown that exercising regularly can lead to a happier, more robust sex life. The American Council on Exercise reports that exercise affects both the mind and body. It improves muscle tone, endurance, and cardiovascular health, and lowers the risk for impotence. Perhaps this is why the Electronic Journal of Human Sexuality concluded that individuals who exercise regularly perceive themselves as more sexually desirable and experience greater levels of sexual satisfaction. Exercise helps you feel happier with your appearance, making you more excited about intimacy. If you and your partner work out together, you'll find you have more sexual energy than ever before.

Stop smoking immediately.

Everyone knows how dangerous smoking is for your health. But did you know that quitting smoking can boost your sex life? Studies have discovered that carbon monoxide affects the production of testosterone, which stifles your sex drive and decreases fertility. Nicotine also tightens blood vessels and restricts blood flow, lessening arousal in women. And because nicotine decreases blood flow to the penis, smoking puts men at risk for impotence. Additionally, smoking affects your appearance, causing unattractive stained teeth, unhealthy skin, wrinkles, and a nasty odor. By quitting smoking, you will instantly be healthier and sexier for your partner. Visit cdc.gov/tobacco to get help quitting.

Introduce something new.

Noted therapist Dagmar O'Connor's 15 years of research led him to write a book that addresses a deeply important topic in every marriage: How to Make Love to the Same Person for the Rest of your Life. O'Connor concludes that a committed, lifelong pair actually have the greatest potential for sex to be "more thrilling, more varied, and more satisfying in every way than any other sexual arrangement you can think of." Experts believe that marriage makes sex easier for people because they are more comfortable, know each other's bodies well, and don't have to travel far for passion. The secret is to introduce something new whenever your sex life starts to feel routine. A new toy, position, or location can spice up your sex life.

Enjoy an intimate getaway.

Making time for sex and intimacy should never feel like a chore on your list of weekly responsibilities. Sometimes, a quick intimate getaway is all you need to recharge your sexual appetite or break out of a rut. Plan a weekend or even just one night without the kids. Find a small, private hotel or bed-and-breakfast that caters to romance. Ignore work responsibilities and shut out all distractions, including email, cell phones, and TV. Relax and enjoy each other's company — schedule a couple's massage, then order room service and champagne. A change of scenery will inspire sex and adventure. You'll head back to reality feeling refreshed, energized, and sexually rejuvenated.

Stay realistic about the ebb and flow of your sex life.

It is completely normal for you or your spouse's sexual appetite to experience highs and lows over the course of your marriage. One partner's decreased interest in sex is not usually an indicator of problems in your relationship. It usually stems more from natural hormonal changes or outside factors. For example, fatigue and stress can kill passion. Additionally, some medications — antidepressants, birth control, and even common-cold remedies — can stifle sex drive. Stay positive through the natural ups and downs of your sex life. Lulls in intimacy will pass. And if you're feeling low, remember — sex is a known stress-reliever!

Ignore the statistics.

On average, married Americans have sex about twice a week. However, as we age, that rate steadily decreases so that married couples 70 and older have sex only about 16 times a year. So how should you and your partner define a "normal" sex life — sex once a month, once a week, or once a day? In truth, "normal" is whatever feels right and satisfies both you and your spouse. The fact is, more sex does not always indicate a happier or healthier marriage. In fact, an AARP study showed that, despite lower frequency of sex, the majority of older married adults are "extremely satisfied" or "somewhat satisfied" with their sex lives. So ignore the statistics and work on cultivating a mutually satisfying sex life.

Seek treatment for sexual problems, either physical or psychological.

In a recent survey, 43 percent of American women and 31 percent of men identified themselves as having a sexual problem. While sexual issues, such as erectile dysfunction, were once believed to be purely mental, more recent data shows that the majority of cases have physical origins, especially as we age. Disease, medication, stress, parenthood, and other factors can cause sexual dysfunction. See a doctor or therapist if you have an ongoing sexual problem. Consulting a professional can help you find the root of the problem and get proper medications and treatment options, as well as peace of mind.

Chapter 20

Managing Finances

Ralph Waldo Emerson once wrote, "Money often costs too much." Indeed, money problems can cost your marriage a great deal — this is why managing finances consistently ranks as the number one cause of marital discord and dissolution, even more than issues involving sex or child-rearing. If you and your spouse come from divergent backgrounds, money may mean very different things to you. You may have incongruent spending habits, dissimilar financial goals, and different attitudes about investing and saving. One of you may be a spender while the other is a saver. The spender may think the saver is cheap. The saver may think the spender is frivolous. To see eye-to-eye on financial matters, you and your spouse must discover what money symbolizes to you both, be it security, power, control, or freedom.

Once you have uncovered your attitudes about money, saving, and spending, you can discuss short- and long-term goals. Use these goals to come up with a budget and financial plan. Creating an effective budget is crucial to managing your money and maintaining a happy union. In recent years, personal bankruptcies have reached an all-time high, with one in every 200 people filing for bankruptcy.

One secret of happy, effective married couples is that they set financial boundaries. They agree to invest and make large purchasing decisions together, always as partners. But making financial decisions as a team does not have to mean sacrificing your financial independence! Happy couples agree on a certain amount of income that each partner may spend at his or her discretion.

Many disagreements or financial mistakes arise because of lack of knowledge. This is why successful couples educate themselves to make sound financial decisions. Working together with a consultant or financial planner is an excellent way to save, spend, and invest wisely. Use this and the following principles to articulate mutual goals, talk through worries, and set realistic financial boundaries so your marriage does not suffer from financial stress.

Talk about your financial differences.

You and your spouse were raised in households that likely took different approaches to money. As a result, you can expect to hold different, and sometimes incompatible, financial attitudes. Some people are natural spenders, while others stretch each dollar to its limit. Ask your spouse how money played a role in his or her family and upbringing; it may clue you in to important attitudes about finances. For example, a person who appears cheap may have grown up with very little money and is thus careful about spending. Talking out your differences will get to the root of your attitudes toward spending and saving, and help put you on the same financial page.

No matter who earns what, make all money decisions together.

Your marriage is a partnership, and all decisions must be made from the standpoint of teammates working toward a common goal. This goes for all financial decisions, regardless of who the breadwinner may be. Just because one partner earns more than the other doesn't mean that he or she should be entitled to, or expected to, make the financial decisions. You and your spouse should do all you can to prevent money from creating an unhealthy imbalance of power in your relationship. Make choices about sales, purchases, investments, and savings as a team — it shows you are both worth the same amount, no matter what you earn.

Assess debts and assets.

Discussing money can be terrifying for many couples, especially when you need to discuss debt. However, a discussion about current debts and assets is imperative to managing your finances. Make a list of what you owe, starting with high-interest debts such as credit cards and student loans. Other debts might include medical bills or car payments. It can be scary to realize how much you owe, but knowing this information is the only way to create an appropriate budget. Next, write down your assets, including cash, stocks, bonds, and investments, such as real estate or the equity of any businesses you have stake in. By assessing your debts and assets, you know where you stand and where you need to go.

Assign money-managing roles.

Your wife might be really good at managing the day-to-day finances and getting the bills paid on time. Your husband may excel at coming up with an overall saving and spending plan. Foster an environment of teamwork by divvying up financial responsibilities according to natural talent and skill. Other important financial jobs include keeping track of incidental spending, doing taxes, looking into health or insurance plans, deciding on investment strategies, choosing charitable contributions, and picking service providers for your utilities. When you assign responsibility for day-to-day money management, bill paying, and other tasks, you eliminate some of the financial stress from your relationship.

Establish long and short-term financial goals.

Before you create a plan for your marital finances, you must decide on mutual long and short-term goals. Long-term goals may be easier to agree upon; they usually include your children's college education, saving for retirement, and paying off debt. Short-term goals may be more of a challenge; you and your spouse may not agree on which ones are most important. For instance, you might discuss taking a family vacation, buying a new car, or remodeling your home. Be honest, assertive, and respectful when discussing your goals. Compromise is crucial. Setting financial goals is the first step in strategizing your money-management plan.

Create a budget.

In the 21st century, the majority of American couples are living beyond their means. In 2007 alone, Americans charged $2.2 trillion in purchases and cash advances on major credit cards. Living beyond your means can threaten the safety of your entire family, so avoid it at all costs. Do so by making a budget that tracks both essential and discretionary expenses. A budget should include items such as household bills, credit obligations, incidentals, discretionary funds, hidden costs, emergency funds, and money for savings or vacations. Creating a budget allows you to evaluate your current spending and make cutbacks or expansions in necessary areas.

Never hide purchases from your spouse.

Don't call your credibility and ability to handle money into question by hiding purchases. It might seem harmless to hide a new golf club or a pair of shoes; however, keeping secrets is not only disrespectful, it interferes with the budget and monetary guidelines you and your spouse worked so hard to establish. And, if the truth surfaces, you may find that you have damaged the trust between you and your spouse. Ask yourself how important that extra purchase really is. Is it important enough to risk damaging your relationship? Make it your policy to be up-front about every purchase you make. If you need more discretionary income, talk to your spouse about it before you make a purchase behind his or her back.

Save money by changing your habits at home.

You don't have to overhaul your entire lifestyle to save money. Talk with your family about simple steps you can all take that will help cut spending in your home. Unplug power adapters when not in use, wash your clothes in cold water, and remember to turn off the lights and ceiling fans when you leave a room. Additionally, make sure your refrigerator is up to date. Old refrigerators cost at least an extra $125 per year to run. Next, change all the light bulbs in your house. Fluorescent bulbs consume 4 times less energy than incandescent bulbs and last 8 times as long. Changing your family's domestic habits is a quick way to save money.

Consult a money-management expert.

You and your partner may be great at your jobs, but neither of you is probably a financial expert. In the same way you hire a mechanic to care for your car, consider hiring a financial advisor to care for your money. Hiring a professional eliminates the stress and confusion that comes with finances. Investment management companies have several portfolios to choose from based on your financial situation and will be available to respond to your questions and concerns. Go to the Financial Planning Association (FPA) for a certified financial planner in your neighborhood or visit the FPA online at www.fpanet.org.

Reevaluate your financial plan periodically.

At least once a year, have a financial check-in with your spouse. Pick a stress-free time and place for this meeting. Use the time to examine your short- and long-term goals. Ask, how did we do last year? What did we do that was successful? Did we stay on budget? Do we need to make some adjustments so we are better able to reach our goals? It is normal to realize that you are off track in one area or another. For example, you may find you spent too much dining out or that you need to save more for your yearly vacation. Make proactive adjustments and look forward to the progress you'll make in the months to come.

Chapter 21

Handling Stress

According to the Centers for Disease Control, the leading 6 causes of death in the U.S. are all brought on at least in part by stress. In addition to shortening your lifespan and putting you at increased risk for disease, stress reduces your quality of life. Stressed people report being more angry, tired, and depressed than non-stressed people. In a marriage, stress occurs from both major life issues or from an accumulation of daily struggles. The big issues, such as job loss, disease, or death, often hit fast and hard. Smaller issues, such as working long hours, not getting enough sleep, daily childcare, or financial worries can hit just as hard, impacting you and your spouse on physical and emotional levels.

Reducing stress is not easy in a fast-paced society like ours. Studies show that Americans are some of the most stressed people on the entire planet. Data from the United Nations indicates that Americans work some of the longest hours of workers in all industrialized countries, while American employers offer some of the poorest vacation plans.

Learning to depend on your spouse and cope with stress is crucial to the success and happiness of your marriage. If you see the signs of stress manifesting themselves in you or your partner — sexual and intimacy problems, frequent arguments, or feeling angry or irritated — take steps to care for yourself both physically and mentally. Sleep, exercise, and nurturing your friendship will help alleviate tension.

It's important to remember that you will need each other most during stressful times. Never push your partner away when you are under stress. Loving relationships are natural stress reducers! (And having emotional support offers you a lower risk of death from stroke, suicide, and heart disease.) If you turn toward one another in times of stress, your marriage can deepen and grow.

Learning to cope with stress as a pair will lead to marital peace and happiness. To this end, use the following principles to get your stress under control.

Nurture your mind and body.

In order to combat stress, you and your partner should nourish your minds and bodies on a daily basis. Get at least 8 hours of sleep a night. Fall asleep without distractions like television. Drink plenty of water during the day. Eat healthy meals that include fresh fruits and vegetables. Exercise together regularly to alleviate tension and rid yourself of stress-inducing hormones. Get out into nature — fresh air will relax and rejuvenate you. Take a fun class together. Be affectionate — you'll be amazed at what a great stress-reducer a hug can be. Spend time with your friends. When you nurture your bodies and minds, stress naturally stays away.

Keep your home neat and organized.

You and your spouse will find that keeping your house clean and organized reduces a great deal of stress. Clutter not only takes up physical space but also negatively affects your mental health. Imagine alleviating the stress that comes from not knowing where to find something or from waking up to a pile of dirty clothes. So, hang your coat up when you take it off. Fold and put away your laundry. Find a permanent place for your keys. Keep bills and important documents in an organized filing system. Have a pen and paper handy near the phone. When you're finished with something, put it back where it belongs. Keeping your surroundings in order will help you and your family live a stress-free life.

Express anger before it boils over.

Frustration, hurt, and rage are directly correlated to stress. Anger, if it is not released, quickly leads to high levels of stress, which jeopardize the quality of your relationship. A Buddhist proverb states, "Holding on to anger is like grasping a hot coal with the intent of throwing it at someone else; you are the one who gets burned." To avoid getting burned, communicate with your partner about the things that irritate you. Talking about it prevents anger from boiling over into a larger problem. If you successfully deal with small annoyances as they come, you can avoid the conflict and stress that result from waiting until you explode with rage.

Relieve stress through meditation.

Meditation can be a wonderful stress-relieving exercise for you as a couple. It can be done easily, quickly, inexpensively, and almost anywhere. Meditation instantly calms you by increasing blood flow and slowing the heart rate, and just 5 minutes of it can have powerful healing and restorative effects. According to the National Institutes of Health, "Meditation techniques offer the potential of learning how to live in an increasingly complex and stressful society while helping to preserve health in the process." So find a quiet spot, sit comfortably, and imagine a peaceful place. Take slow, deep breaths. Clear your mind of all stressors. In no time, meditation may become your favorite way to relax with your spouse!

185

Stick to your budget.

According to the American Psychological Association, 73 percent of Americans list money as the number one factor that affects their stress level. Therefore, creating and sticking to a budget will help you and your partner avoid stressful situations that negatively impact your marriage. If you cannot afford to purchase something nonessential with cash, don't buy it. Put items on your credit cards only when you know you can pay off the whole balance when you receive the bill. Sticking to your budget may mean you can't have a new outfit or the latest technology, but you will enjoy the peace of mind that comes with not being in debt.

Avoid becoming a workaholic.

Writer Margaret Fuller once noted, "Men for the sake of getting a living forget to live." Being a workaholic will not only stress you out, but will reduce your time with your family and place undue stress on your home life. If you find yourself devoting inordinate chunks of time to work, remember that your family and marriage are ultimately more important than your job. Refrain from working more than 9 hours a day and keep at least one day a week completely work-free. The world is not likely to fall apart if you do not check your email or return a phone call immediately, so there is no sense in adding such stress to your life.

Don't take it personally when your partner reacts to stress.

Everyone has times in which they succumb to stress. For one person, this may mean being grumpy, argumentative, or especially aggressive; for someone else, it may mean withdrawing, being moody, or extremely fatigued. Should your partner exhibit signs of stress, try not to take it personally. Instead of getting upset, step aside and grant your partner space to decompress. Ask if you can do anything to help — sometimes being offered a glass of water or a snack is enough to cut through your partner's tension. The stressed mood will likely pass in a few minutes, and you will have avoided an unnecessary fight.

Look for solutions to stress, not a temporary escape.

An old saying goes, "Vacation is what you take when you can't take what you've been taking any longer." When you and your spouse are suffering from stress, resist the urge to take a vacation, as the moment you return home, the anxiety will be back. Indeed, escaping from stress ensures it will always be a part of your life. The key is to find the source of the stress and remove it for good.

Look for what is causing your stress. Is there a tool you might use to get organized? Is there an area in which you might cut back? Can you eliminate one responsibility you've taken on? Create solutions to your stressors and you'll have found long-term relief.

Don't be afraid to admit when you're in over your head.

Don't be afraid to admit when you and your spouse have taken on more than you can handle. Perhaps you're tackling a complicated home-improvement project that has taken on a life of its own. Or, perhaps you are like many couples who overextend themselves socially and suddenly have a booked calendar that is exhausting simply to look at. If you have overcommitted yourselves, call on friends, in-laws, or neighbors for help. Learn how to say no so in the future you feel less stressed. Knowing how and when to say no is important to managing your stress levels and keeping your marriage happy and harmonious.

Practice healthy skills for coping with stress.

Football legend Paul Brown once said, "The key to winning is poise under stress." Likewise, the key to "winning" happiness in your marriage is to learn skills that help you and your partner cope with stress. First, give you and your spouse permission to express emotions related to stress. Cry, or yell at the top of your lungs for 10 seconds if you need to. Next, find someone other than your spouse to vent to when you feel overwhelmed, or, keep a journal. Finally, plan to do something as a couple that will be completely stress-free, such as eating dinner out, taking a relaxing walk, or watching a funny movie.

Chapter 22

Planning for Your Future

By now, you've learned many ways to bond, communicate, enrich your partnership, resolve conflict, ignite your sex life, and grow together as a married couple.

Whether you're in the "honeymoon stage" (the stage of marriage in which everything is new and exciting, and intimacy is at an all-time high), the "reality stage" (you are reevaluating some of your expectations of marriage), the "accommodation stage" (you are learning to manage one another's needs and differences and investing in healthy ways of communicating), or the "transformation and success stage" (you have weathered many storms and have a shared legacy), you always have opportunities for profound growth and connection. As you grow, it is important to look ahead to your future as a couple. Successfully planning for your future means being prepared to weather both the winters and summers of your marriage.

Planning for the future requires you to have patience, be optimistic, and also be realistic about your marriage. When you plan for your future together, imagine that the best is yet to come. When you dream, plan for an abundance of happiness, security, and adventure, and do not limit yourself. Be confident in your plan and in the knowledge that you have the tools to navigate the difficult times. Be flexible with your marriage, and understand that even the best-laid plans can change. Unforeseen roadblocks will appear in your marital path, so be prepared to deal with the shifts and changes that make up life.

American journalist William Allen White once wrote, "I am not afraid of tomorrow, for I have seen yesterday, and I love today." Although planning for your marital future can be complex and even a little frightening, trust that your future will be as good, or even better, than your relationship has been thus far. Whether you're discussing having children, moving to a new city, buying a home, starting a business, or retirement, be excited about what is next for you and your partner. The following principles will help you create a successful plan for the future of your happy, healthy union.

Big Idea

191

Make a list of the things you want to do in your lifetime.

Together with your spouse, create a list of things you want to do in your lifetime. Some will be simple, such as "try a new cuisine" or "camp out under the stars." Others may call for some planning, such as "plant a garden," "get to know our neighbors," or "build a wine collection." Still other things on your list will require lots of foresight and preparation, such as "hike through a rainforest," "visit the Great Wall of China," or "learn to scuba dive." The wonderful part of this exercise is you get to dream together and plan for future adventures. Don't limit yourselves, as you have your entire lives to complete everything on your list.

Prepare yourselves to have children.

There are countless things to consider when preparing to transition from being a couple to a family. The most important is whether you are actually ready for one! Are you ready to be completely selfless, sacrifice personal time, vacations, and even career plans? Are you prepared to pay for a stroller, car seat, baby food, clothes, and diapers? The Department of Agriculture reports that a child costs about $10,000 a year. Have you talked about the added strain on your marriage that a child will create? Having a family means less time to spend alone, connecting and working on your marriage. Prepare yourself for having children by discussing these important issues.

Visualize yourselves in 5, 10, 25, and 50 years.

Imagine you and your spouse's life in 5, 10, 25, and 50 years. What do you envision? What would be your ideal circumstance? Where might you live? What kinds of things will you have? Will you be parents? Homeowners? Career moguls? Where might you retire? What physical shape might you be in? How you imagine yourselves at different points throughout life is the first step to making goals happen. Furthermore, picturing yourselves together, even after decades, helps strengthen your bond as life partners. As a pair, revisit your visions periodically to make sure you are still seeing the same things.

Plan for retirement.

You and your spouse will work hard for many years, and eventually you will need a break. To this end, plan for a comfortable, happy retirement. The sooner you start the better; financial analysts agree that retirees will need to save about $1 million in order to retire comfortably at age 65 and live for another 30 years. For young working couples, T. Rowe Price recommends trying to save 15 percent of your gross salaries. A great place to start is by enrolling in a company 401(k) or 403(b) plan. Also, consult your financial planner about investing in IRA funds, and cut back on discretionary spending. Being able to retire comfortably is crucial to your continued happiness as a married couple.

Big Idea

195

Plan for the care of your elderly family members.

In the U.S., people 65 or older make up 12.6 percent of the population. As your parents and other relatives age, you and your spouse will need to plan for their care, which can be a complicated endeavor. There are a few basic options for elder care. The family member can remain independent and live on his or her own with the help of a home nurse; extended family can take the elderly person into their home; or the elderly family member can be placed into an assisted-living facility. You want your elderly family members to be as safe and comfortable as possible, so it's important to talk to them and plan for the best arrangement.

196

Plan to take care of your family through estate planning.

Although no one wants to talk about death, you and your spouse need to consider how your family and finances will be taken care of when you pass away. Estate planning includes drafting a will, assigning power of attorney, creating a living will or medical power of attorney, and, for many people, opening a trust. Consult a professional to help you take inventory of your assets and determine who you want to inherit them. Also, figure out who you want to make medical decisions if you are unable to. Estate planning is a difficult but necessary part of planning for your family's future.

Cherish your past.

An important aspect of creating a happy and healthy future together is cherishing the good times of your past. A shared history is a wonderful predecessor to a successful tomorrow. With this in mind, pass on family stories to your children. Tell them stories about your marriage — the day you and your spouse met, your first date, your wedding day, and the moment you learned the two of you were becoming parents. As a couple, document and relive all the amazing experiences you have had together. Remember all you have witnessed, created, and survived. Create journals, photo albums, scrapbooks, and home videos. Cherishing your past will help you look forward to what is still to come.

Have faith in your ability to navigate your future.

Philosopher Rabindranath Tagore once said, "Faith is the bird that feels the light when the dawn is still dark." Indeed, putting trust in the existence of what you cannot see is difficult at times, but very important to the future of your marriage. Believing in a grand plan will help you understand the chaos of life and will help you through the hard times. A proverb states, "Faith is like electricity — we cannot see it, but we can see the light." In truth, there is evidence of the divine in your marriage every day — but you must be looking for it. You and your spouse must believe in your strength and stay faithful that you can navigate the unknown together.

Prepare for the unexpected.

Misfortune befalls everyone now and then, whether it be the average annoyances of everyday life or unexpected catastrophes. From frustrating coworkers and a broken washing machine to job loss, illness, and death, you and your spouse must have a plan for the unexpected. Keep up-to-date emergency contact information around your home in case of a natural disaster. Have money set aside for emergencies or sudden job loss; the equivalent of 3 months salary or more is recommended. Have a plan for how to handle responsibilities should one partner become sick or incapacitated. Perhaps the best way to prepare for the unexpected is to adopt a positive attitude and learn to smile through adversity.

Renew your vows

Renewing your wedding vows is a wonderful, meaningful way for you and your partner to celebrate your past and future. Renewing your vows allows you to reflect on and celebrate how far you've come and where you are going as a couple. Many couples renew their vows at certain marriage milestones, such as their 10th, 25th, or 50th anniversaries. You can have a large party, a small family affair, or even a formal wedding ceremony. Make the day special by rewriting your vows and reading them aloud. After renewing your vows, your marriage will surely feel reinvigorated. As the poet Robert Browning wisely wrote, "Grow old along with me, the best is yet to be."

Chapter 23

Conclusion

Congratulations! After reading this book you should feel great about your ability to enrich your marriage so that it remains happy and healthy for a lifetime. While it won't always be easy, the best way to help a struggling marriage or improve a great one is by applying the principles in this book. If you constantly argue, read up on ways to deal with and avoid conflict; if you struggle to communicate, learn the techniques of active listening; if you've lost the passion in your marriage, jot down a few simple ways to put romance, affection, and spontaneity back in your daily life. This book contains the basic pillars of all happy and healthy marriages and provides you with more than 200 other ideas, tips, tricks, and pieces of advice for having a fulfilling lifelong partnership.

The Little Book of Big Ideas for a Happy and Healthy Marriage gives you the tools to deal with the increasingly difficult odds against having a lasting relationship. It also gives you hundreds of reasons why you will want to work on improving your marriage daily, despite how daunting it might sometimes seem.

As you apply the wisdom in this book to solidify your marriage, it is important to remember that every day you are changing your lives, your family, and your community for the better. Some of these benefits will be seen immediately. Other changes will take longer to realize, but they are just as important to pursue. No matter which aspects of your marriage need the most work, know that your daily hard work will pay off, and your love will continue to blossom!

Most important, you must practice what you have learned in this book often in order to continue to learn and grow as a married couple. Keep this book handy and refer to it when you and your spouse need a reminder, pick-me-up, or words of inspiration. And above all, remember that the single greatest gift you can give each other, and your family, is that of a happy and healthy marriage.